OPENING MY EYES UNDER WATER

OPENING MY EYES UNDER WATER

Essays on Hope, Humanity, and Our Hero Michelle Obama

ASHLEY WOODFOLK

FEIWEL AND FRIENDS

NEW YORK

A Feiwel and Friends Book
An imprint of Macmillan Publishing Group, LLC
120 Broadway, New York, NY 10271 • fiercereads.com

Our books may be purchased in bulk for promotional, educational, or
business use. Please contact your local bookseller or the Macmillan
Corporate and Premium Sales Department at (800) 221-7945 ext. 5442
or by email at MacmillanSpecialMarkets@macmillan.com.

Library of Congress Cataloging-in-Publication Data is available.

First edition, 2022
Book design by Mallory Grigg
Feiwel and Friends logo designed by Filomena Tuosto
Printed in the United States of America

ISBN 978-1-250-24037-8 (hardcover)
10 9 8 7 6 5 4 3 2 1

For Mommy.
The First Lady of my heart.

OPENING MY EYES UNDER WATER

Step out of your
comfort zones and soar.

—MICHELLE OBAMA,
Howard University speech, 2016

FOREWORD

EVERYONE HAS BEEN ASKED THE QUESTION in a hundred different iterations by the time they reach high school. It had happened to me so often, in fact, that after having to write what felt like a million essays about it as a kid, I hadn't sat down and thought about it in years.

Who is your biggest role model? a worksheet from fifth grade probably read. *Who do you aspire to be like?* my eighth-grade English teacher may have scrawled across the whiteboard. *If you could have dinner with anyone, alive or dead, who would it be and why?* a college admissions essay for my safety school begged to know. But once I did think about it again, once I focused my energy the way I used to when I was asked about (what I considered to be) arbitrary nonsense by adults who just wanted to keep me busy, I realized why the question was so salient and why it had been asked again and again. I could finally see why it was important for young me to take a second and consider who I might want to model my life after.

The reason role models are important, and the truth your teachers don't want to tell you, are one and the same: **No one knows what the hell they're doing.** Not any of the adults in your life; not your seemingly perfect older siblings or the most put-together juniors and seniors; not even your heroes. Take comfort in the fact that we're all just making it up as we go along—making the best choices we can with the information we have at the time. We're making it work. But what those people do have is a few more years of experience. They've made mistakes they'd rather not see you repeat. So, emulating someone whose life looks like what you hope yours one day will is sometimes incredibly helpful.

I think about all those essay questions a little differently now. Instead of assuming adults were giving me a pointless assignment to "keep me busy," I think that maybe they were trying to guide me. Maybe they were attempting to help me find the keys to the car of my life and give me a little direction. If I had the chance to rewrite any of those essays now, I'd pick a human most people would think was totally cliché. I'd pick someone whom I could write a whole book about. I'd pick someone like Michelle Obama.

Something tells me that choice would be a

good one, if only because the internet is littered with roundups of Michelle Obama's quotations. There are lists pulled from her autobiography, *Becoming*; lists that are a compilation of wise words from her speeches; and even sound bites from some of her most viral interviews. But regardless of when or how these words entered our collective consciousness, one thing has always been true: We collect Michelle Obama's words because even though she too has had moments where she didn't know what the hell she was doing, her life has had an incredible trajectory. Despite the confusion and cluelessness inherent in being human, Michelle is a maverick.

She has lived an utterly remarkable life full of as much unexpected opportunity as confidently executed choices; with as many exhilarating twists and turns as massive, independently built successes. Many, including me, feel that she is extraordinary, and not just because she happened to marry the man who would go on to become America's first Black president. Though perhaps something can be said for the fact that she saw something exceptional in him—that the same magnetism that could attract and sustain the attention and love of a bright, ambitious, and nearly unstoppable young woman may have been part of the reason he landed in the White House. Michelle Obama is a brilliant thinker and creative in her own right, and I've sought out her words when I was looking for encouragement or a confidence boost before making an intimidating decision in my own life, so much so that an inner refrain became *What would Michelle do?* Or sometimes: *What would she say?*

Just as I did when I was younger, I still

sometimes find myself feeling lost or over-whelmed or unsure if I'm doing the right thing. And because I didn't know Michelle Obama existed until I had graduated from college, I didn't have her words to call upon (and I didn't have her as a go-to answer for all those essay questions) as early as I wish I had.

This book is a reimagining of that: of how I might have applied Michelle's wisdom to my life had I encountered it sooner. It's a love letter to a strong, sensitive, incredibly humble but still heroic Black woman whom generations of women now have the privilege to admire. And it's a meditation on what I and so many others have in common with one of the most aspirational and inspirational role models of our time.

I'm sure Michelle would say anyone could

accomplish the things she has with the right set of circumstances, opportunities, and preparation, but I know how hard something like that can be to believe. My hope is that with this book, you'll see that achieving a life you're proud of, a life that others might even one day aspire to emulate, isn't as impossible as it might seem. My hope is that through reading, you'll see just how capable you are, how powerful you can be, and how much you have in common with the indomitable Michelle Obama. And maybe with me too.

Every "role model" was a kid once. Every "role model" has regrets. Every "role model" is as human as you and I. Even Michelle Obama. And still, they blossomed.

You will too.

Failure is an important
part of your growth and
development of resilience.
Don't be afraid to fail.

—MICHELLE OBAMA,
speech at Apollo Theater, 2015

I DON'T FAIL.

Or maybe I should say that I've never been okay with failing. I'm a semi-reformed perfectionist—one who was once so hell-bent on being perfect that I preferred to give up on things than to try my best and potentially fail at them.

I quit swim lessons when I was six. One Saturday morning during free swim at the end of class, the teacher explained that we'd have to go underwater and open our eyes without goggles at the next lesson to recover something from below the surface. I went home and told my mother I wasn't doing that. The chlorine would sting, and why would I put myself through unnecessary pain when Olympic swimmers could wear goggles and I never went to the pool or beach without mine? I couldn't think of a reason or situation in which this skill would be one I'd need, and deep down I doubted my ability to keep my unprotected eyes open long enough underwater to retrieve the rings my teacher would drop into the pool for us to find. My mother asked the teacher if I could still wear my goggles, but she said no. So, I refused to go back.

I quit ballet when I was eight and a half because a ballerina came to my class and showed us what her feet looked like. She explained that when you get pointe shoes, you lose toenails and develop corns and bunions and that even breaking a toe or two is normal. I was afraid I wouldn't be able to deal with the pain—that the second I tried to go on pointe and it hurt too badly or the dancers around me succeeded before I could, I would feel like an untalented loser. I loved dancing, I thought, so I should quit before pointe shoes were handed out and broken in. I should go before everyone could be better than I'd ever be.

I went on to quit the saxophone and the clarinet, chorus, basketball, and competitive cheerleading, though I stuck that out the longest despite feeling like I wasn't as good or as flexible as the other girls. I even wanted to quit when I was learning to drive because I couldn't figure out how to parallel park. And on and on it went.

At the same time, I stuck with the things I did well, the things I knew I had to do to keep up my veneer of perfection. I got excellent grades. I was an officer in student government. I was on the yearbook and prom committees, and I was in poetry club. I had the list of colleges I wanted to apply to finalized by sophomore year. I aced tests and signed up for AP classes, worked and went to church every Sunday with my family, and was a "good girl," always making it home before curfew. I met everyone's expectations, almost always.

As I read Michelle Obama's memoir, I deeply related to her description of herself as a "box checker." She writes that she got good grades and applied to the best schools and remained laser-focused on her goals. She wasn't, as she called it, "a swerver." And despite my streak of quitting, I was the same way. Some might have seen me as a quitter, but I saw myself as someone unwilling to take unnecessary risks. Why risk failing when I knew I could excel at so many other, more important things?

But I wasn't exactly happy. I was always anxious and overwhelmed, and working so hard to be seen as perfect when I was so far from that ideal was exhausting. Similarly, Michelle had painted herself into a corner. She'd become the person she thought she was supposed to be—the person she thought everyone else expected her to be. And it wasn't until she experienced major loss— the death of a close friend and her father—that she realized where all that box checking had landed her. She was "successful," but at what cost?

When Michelle met Barack, she was at this crossroads. And meeting someone whose life had followed such an untraditional path inspired her to ask herself a new question. Instead of thinking about who everyone else expected her to be, Michelle was able to ask herself: Who do *I* want to be?

She went on to take some big risks, including a huge career change for herself, and of course eventually agreeing to support her husband's decision to pursue politics. And in a swerve to end all swerves—his running for president of the United States—Michelle encountered the largest risk she'd ever taken. She was risking her very lucrative career, her children's futures, and the life she'd imagined for herself all at once.

My crossroads came when I decided to listen to a whisper that had always been inside me, but that I'd buried again and again because the risk of failing was too great: I wanted to be a writer. This would be my big swerve—the first and perhaps only big risk I'd ever been brave enough to take. And I would (and did) fail. A lot.

Take, for instance, this very book. This is not

the book I set out to write. If you scroll back through miles of my Twitter feed, you'll see just how true that is. A very different book was announced ages ago, one that was intended to be a biography of the Obamas—both Michelle and Barack—and one I tried and failed to complete for nearly two years, spanning the pregnancy and birth of my first kid, my departure from a professional career in publishing, the COVID-19 pandemic, unprecedented civil and racial unrest, and the worst mental health months I've had in my whole life.

During this time, and with the help of therapy, I realized my fear of failure came from a fear of vulnerability. I had never written a book like the one I was attempting, and trying to do things I've never done before always puts me in a very vulnerable position: a place where someone could say "you suck" and it might be true. It was the same way I'd felt as a kid when I'd been so afraid of failing—of opening my eyes underwater, going on pointe, playing a new instrument or sport—that I'd quit. Feeling incompetent or inadequate is a very dangerous way to feel if you're someone, like I was, who ties their self-worth directly to how good or bad they are at everything.

I feared if people found out I wasn't perfect, they'd figure out I wasn't valuable. And if I wasn't valuable, was I worthy of their time, or more importantly, their love?

(The secret was, everyone already knew I wasn't perfect. The secret was, I was loved and accepted anyway.)

But back to the book.

I wanted to quit, but I didn't. And because that book just would not and could not work—not for me, not at the time, not in the world as it existed—I had to admit it: I had tried, and I had failed.

When my editors and I realized the book wasn't working, we had a few conversations about why, and then decided to pivot—to move in a new and different direction. As I'd been researching the original book, I'd collected a ton of quotes by both Michelle and Barack, and I kept being drawn to Michelle's, especially any that were about success and self-love and resilience.

The quote that opens this essay, about failure and growth, was one that had always stuck with me. I couldn't shake the assertion that I would only grow and get better every time I failed at something. It was revolutionary, this idea that I was *inherently valuable*, even when I wasn't perfect. That perhaps imperfection was a good thing—it would help me grow.

If you're anything like me, anything like Michelle, or even the exact opposite of a box checker, I want to make sure you hear this, so I'll say it again: **You are inherently valuable, even when you are not perfect.**

So, this book will not be perfect because, despite my tireless efforts to overcome my own humanity, I am not perfect. But I will be honest. And I will be open. And I hope you find some courage in these pages all the same. I hope you'll be as touched and inspired by Michelle Obama's words as I have been.

I'm no longer quitting when I'm afraid I will

fail. I'm jumping into the pool with both eyes open, lacing up those pointe shoes, sitting down at my computer with my heart in my hands.

I'm listening to Michelle, and I'm being brave with the hope that I'll come out the other side more resilient for it. This may be a fiasco, but this is, as Mary Oliver wrote, my "one wild and precious life." I'm done with checking boxes. I'm taking so many beautiful, terrifying risks.

I am still afraid, but I'm doing it all anyway.

Your story is what you
have, what you'll always have.
It is something to own.

—MICHELLE OBAMA,
Becoming

MY STORY STARTS THE WAY MOST STORIES do: with me not knowing what the hell I was doing but thinking that I knew everything.

Of course, I was born at a certain time in a certain place and into a certain family, and of course all those things had profound effects on the way I live and move through the world, but whenever anyone asks to hear "my story," I rarely start before the year I was twelve.

Twelve is an interesting age. Even as an adult I'd assert that being twelve was the worst year of my life (and I doubt that I'm alone). Partially because, as I mentioned, I didn't know what I was doing while assuming I knew everything, but also because it was the first time I felt like I was my own person; that I didn't have the complete protection of my parents; that I was a bit on my own. But also, being twelve is just really, *really* hard.

The year I turned twelve was the year I got my period, the year I had my first intensely painful crush, the year I got braces, and the year I got boobs. As if all of that wasn't enough to chip away at my little preteen soul, it was also the year I was targeted by a bully for the first time in my life.

Bullying is fascinating because it is essentially someone else deciding to tell the world who they think you are. It is someone deciding that, for whatever reason, you don't have a say in your own story, and instead they attempt to narrate, dictate, and change your story themselves. Bullies take power away from their victims by editing the narrative of someone else's existence to whatever they want it to be. ("You're weak," "You're dumb," "You're ugly," "You're worthless.") And it's painful because they're always wrong. The story they're telling either misrepresents their victim completely or only tells a fraction of the truth, which they twist and skew to cause the maximum amount of pain.

Keep this in mind. We'll come back to it later.

Before the seventh grade, I'd experienced some light bullying. I had been called a few names in elementary school because I was so skinny and awkward; because I spoke, as some put it, "like a white girl;" because despite those things I was still bright and loud and someone who took up space. I still had lots of friends and was largely well liked. Despite the occasional hurt feelings, I mostly ignored the meanness as it came and went.

Fast forward to middle school. In seventh grade, I fell in with a group of four other girls. We naturally gravitated to each other, though when I think about it now, I'm not sure why. Maybe it was just proximity since we were all "smart" kids on the talented and gifted track. Maybe it was something else. But that year, the year I turned twelve, was the first time I had a bona fide bully. One of the girls in my new "friend" group was intent on making my life hell. For whatever reason, she decided I was her target, and she went after me, relentlessly, daily.

She made fun of my clothes, the way I spoke, the music I liked. If I dared to answer a question in class, she'd swear I was sucking up to the teacher. She said I thought I was better than everyone if my parents picked me up early or because of what they packed in my lunch. With her words, she changed me from the person I knew myself to be—someone who liked to wear bright colors; who was caring and excitable; who loved to read and was open-minded, well cared for, and interested in everything—into someone who kissed teachers' asses, was stuck up, and had bad taste.

She also teased me about my body. I was lithe and long-limbed and essentially curveless until breasts sprang forth out of nowhere, making me incredibly self-conscious. Then, in addition to being targeted by her, I was incessantly and inappropriately touched by boys. Another narrative popped up then too that had nothing to do with who I actually was: that because I suddenly had boobs, I must have been having sex. I must have wanted the attention, because if I didn't, why was

I wearing those tiny, tight T-shirts? Why were my bra straps showing unless I wanted someone to snap them? The truth was, my body changed so suddenly I didn't know how to outfit it. My clothes got tighter so quickly I barely noticed. In retrospect, perhaps she was jealous of my body, because I was skinnier than she was, my breasts appearing larger than they actually were because the rest of me hadn't caught up yet. Either way, she told stories about me that had nothing to do with me. And for a while, I didn't know what to do about it. I told no one because I thought I could handle it. I had no clue what I was doing, but I thought I knew everything.

Though Barack Obama has mentioned being bullied as a kid because of his name and his big ears, because of being one of only a few Black kids at his prestigious private school in Hawaii, Michelle Obama wasn't bullied in exactly the same way. At least not as constantly as her husband and I were as kids and preteens. She was teased for talking "white" (the same way I was), she was accused of being stuck up (the same way I was), and her peers sought to make her feel inferior because they were intimidated by her height and confidence and smarts. She felt unsure of how to balance being both brilliant and Black because so many people pretended as if those things were mutually exclusive, but Michelle suffered no fools, even as a kid, so I think the insults largely didn't stick. However, once she and Barack began to campaign for the presidency, they were bullied on an entirely different level.

Their stories were co-opted by numerous

bullies, some taking the form of media outlets or newscasters; some were their fellow politicians, and even regular citizens who had large platforms they used to twist facts about the Obamas to fit the narrative they hoped to spread. It started with the "birther" movement—individuals and national groups who spread misinformation about where Barack Obama was born. It continued with suggestions that he practiced Islam—which was only able to gain traction because of the rampant Islamophobia that exists in the United States— that he was a terrorist sympathizer, and that he and his family were just generally unpatriotic and unfit to represent the American people.

A few of the most insidious incidents of the harassment will forever stick out in my memory. Shortly before delivering his victory speech after being named the 2008 Democratic candidate for president, Barack shared a fist bump onstage with Michelle—an innocent expression of congratulations and excitement. A Fox News anchor, E. D. Hill, referred to it on-air as a "terrorist fist bump."

I can't forget the times when Michelle Obama herself became a target of this bullying and harassment before her husband even became president. One such moment came on the campaign trail when Michelle said, "For the first time in my adult lifetime, I am really proud of my country." Conservatives jumped to use this statement as proof that the Obamas (and especially Michelle) were un-American; to change their story and paint them as too liberal and too different from the average American citizen to be the country's First Family.

And then there was the blatant racism. The political cartoons that depicted Michelle with overly masculine features, or that mentioned watermelon or chicken. The open disrespect that came in the form of name-calling or behaviors meant to belittle or delegitimize Barack. And the myth of a post-racial America after his victory that served to make everyone less willing to acknowledge that America was still very much a country that preferred whiteness, tradition, and exclusivity to Blackness, diversity, and inclusivity.

I am hesitant to draw a direct parallel between what happened to me in middle school and the Obamas' bullying, which was largely racially motivated, and which existed on a national scale. And in a lot of ways, they aren't remotely similar. What happened to me was tiny and specific, and in the grand scheme of the history of the world, perhaps it was even insignificant. What happened to the Obamas affected an entire generation—and it will exist in books written about those years forever. But when you're twelve, and someone's goal becomes solely to make you as unhappy as possible, it becomes a huge part of your personal history, even if it isn't in history books. And ultimately, losing control of your own story is always detrimental, whether the world is watching or not.

For years, other people, mostly in the media, told the Obamas' story for them. In op-eds and think pieces, novelizations and movies, even interviews where actual words the Obamas spoke were framed in ways they didn't expect or perhaps didn't agree with. And they dealt with it, mostly by ignoring the incessant storytellers and only discounting the most egregious rumors, or those that involved harmful lies about people they loved and respected.

Eventually, once the former president's two terms had ended and the family had left the White House for the last time, they each took steps to reclaim their stories completely. In 2018, Michelle Obama released *Becoming*, a retelling of her entire life, including her perspective of the eight years her husband spent in office, and a couple of years later Barack Obama followed with *A Promised Land* (a third installment to two prior memoirs of his), with more volumes planned in coming years.

Of course, we can't all write entire books every time we get bullied. Or, I mean, we *could*, but we shouldn't have to. There's a very easy shortcut we can all take. The way we can own our stories, as Michelle Obama insists we must, is this: We decide who we are and we move through the world in a way that is aligned with that truth. It was what I did in the seventh grade, though sadly it took me most of the school year to drum up the courage to stop shrinking from my bully's abuse. I didn't have any kind of official standoff with her the way victims of bullying always have in movies, but I did start wearing the things that I liked to wear, raising my hand in class to answer questions again, and reaching out to a few new girls to be friends with. I slowly distanced myself from her, and by the time eighth grade started, she no longer seemed to be getting any satisfaction out of bullying me, because everyone could clearly see that the things she was saying about me simply weren't true.

When people—whether those people are our parents, bullies, the media, or anyone else—try to redefine us in their own terms, we must defy their lies with every move we make. And I don't mean that we alter our behavior to counter their distortions of who we are—I mean that we live so authentically that anyone paying any real attention would immediately see the truth.

We own our stories by living our truths; by telling the world who we are every day and by being our fullest selves. When we do this, all the rumors and false narratives will eventually fall away. And even if they linger in the minds of a few intent on misunderstanding us—we know what's real. Our story will be ours to tell for anyone willing to listen. As Michelle Obama has also said, "You don't have to say anything to the haters. You don't have to acknowledge them at all. You just wake up every morning and be the best you, you can be. And that tends to shut them up."

SIDE NOTE: ON "TALKING WHITE"

When I called my college roommate to introduce myself and so we could discuss who was bringing what to our shared dorm room, I was extremely preoccupied with somehow letting her know that I was Black.

This was before the days of Instagram and smartphones. Facebook wasn't even a thing yet, so there was no way for her to know unless I told her.

You see, you can't hear my voice right now, but if you could, you would probably conclude that my voice belonged to a white woman. My voice is high-pitched and clear, youthful, and vibrant. My pronunciation and rhythm and most of the time even my word choice don't betray or portray my race. And when a voice like mine is coupled with the name Ashley, information my new college roommate *did* have, I knew she'd be expecting a white girl on move-in day unless I made it abundantly clear that I was, in fact, not white at all.

I settled on asking her what she looked like, "you know, so I can recognize you on the first day," I added with false enthusiasm, when in reality, I was a nervous wreck. After she told me she was "around 5'5" and blond," I took a deep breath and casually mentioned I was Black. "You know, typical Black girl," I think I said. "Brown skin, brown hair, and brown eyes."

But why, you might be wondering, was this something I had to worry about? And more importantly: Why was "talking white" something that both Michelle and I were teased about? Why was the way I sounded problematic around both white and Black people?

Let's start with why I was worried. College was the first time in my life I'd be in a setting that was majority white, so I didn't know what to expect. I'd grown up in Washington, DC, attended predominantly Black public schools, and my parents had attended a historically Black college, so pretty much everyone in my life was non-white. My mother even said the only reason she cried after they dropped me off at my dorm was because she felt like she was leaving me with strangers (the strangeness only being the whiteness of my chosen university). Since I had no experience with white people, I didn't know how they would be. I didn't know how they would experience an encounter with me. I instinctively felt I had to protect myself from my white roommate expecting a white girl, because (1) "white" is the accepted and expected default human, (2) there is a long history of white people assuming they know how Black people "sound," and (3) I didn't want to have to *see* her reaction to being surprised about my race. I wanted her to know who I was so that if she had any issue with my Blackness, it could be dealt with before I was standing in the room with her.

Luckily we had no trouble, but ironically the very thing I was afraid of experiencing happened to Michelle Obama at Princeton.

Unbeknownst to her at the time, her roommate (or at least her roommate's mother) was not okay with Michelle being Black. The girl's mother contacted the school repeatedly until her daughter was relocated. Of course Michelle remembered the girl's departure, but it wasn't until later that she found out why.

I should also mention that once I was at school, people made all kinds of assumptions about me and microaggressions toward me related to how I spoke. Things like assuming I went to private school, or making fun of the few words I did pronounce with a "Blaccent." One time someone even asked if I was adopted—by white people, of course—with the implication being I spoke too well to have a Black family.

And now for the issue of both Michelle and me being teased for "talking white": Black kids only weaponize speech because the dominant culture, whiteness, weaponized it against us first. I could get into the storied history of what is accepted as "proper" speaking or "correct English," and how it was and is purposefully used to withhold opportunities from minorities. I could explain how African American Vernacular English, also known as AAVE, has all the same rules as a fully formed language because it *is* a fully formed language that is recognized and studied by linguists, but it has never been viewed as such by the average person because of white supremacy and the fact that Black people are the people who speak it. I could dive into the legacy of criminalized Black literacy (it was literally illegal to teach Black people to read and write) and "separate but equal" schooling that was not equal at all, and how having a certain name and a certain way of speaking can be the difference between getting a job and not getting one simply because of systemic racism.

I could write about how I heard my mother code-switch whenever she had to make business calls and the difference was so jarring we all laughed about it, and how she so adamantly didn't want me to have to change my speech at will, so she drilled into me the importance of articulation. She knew that my having a certain voice would directly contribute to my level of opportunity and potential success. Michelle and

I were probably teased about the way we spoke because kids have a tendency to shun anything that makes someone different. But suffice it to say that this particular issue has a very long and dark history.

The point of all this is that the way you sound has very little to do with who you are. It means nothing about your abilities, your smarts, or what you have to offer. But white supremacy is a system built on exclusion that would have us all believe otherwise.

Code-switching shouldn't have to exist, but it does in response to a system that was created to exclude immigrants, the poor, and Black people, and benefit those who are rich, educated, and white. So while I wish you didn't have to, code-switch if you need to—it is fine to do what you must in a society designed the way ours is. But just remember that it is a *design*; a system that was made up by powerful people so that they could keep the power they had and gain more by not allowing others to prosper. It is a *design*. It is not the truth.

There is no such thing as "talking white."

Friendships between women,
as any woman will tell you, are built
of a thousand small kindnesses . . .
swapped back and forth and over again.

—MICHELLE OBAMA,

Becoming

IN SEVENTH GRADE, DURING MAYBE MY third period ever, I was in the bathroom of my junior high school changing my pad between classes.

I don't know if you've ever been in a middle school girls' bathroom, but it's like the fucking Hunger Games in there. Girls are putting on makeup and talking shit about other girls and painting their nails and screaming about who likes who and maybe someone is even getting their ass kicked.

Anyway, it's a scary place, and it's the last place you'd ever want to do or say something embarrassing. Teenage and preteen girls are like moths to a flame when it comes to moments of embarrassment—they swarm, and they almost never let you live it down. With no teachers around, things went south in girls' bathrooms fast.

As I said, it was maybe my third period ever. I was still too nervous to use a tampon, and I was a heavy bleeder, so I had these huge pads. As I was taking the old one off and before I could put the new one on, I dropped it, and it landed used side up in the space between my stall and the one next to me.

I was instantly mortified, and I froze, waiting for someone to scream, "Ew!", for all twenty-plus girls who were in the bathroom to turn and stare, for my new name to be Bloody Mary or something equally as humiliating.

Luckily, before the worst could unfold, a friend who happened to be in the next stall over whispered my name and kicked the pad back to me. Her voice broke the spell and I grabbed it and quickly got rid of it. I'm sure she thought nothing of it at the time and probably doesn't even remember that it happened, but I've never forgotten that kindness.

I can name countless other moments, tiny and huge, in which I or a friend shared a kindness like that one. Everything from swapping pieces of advice to sharing secrets or borrowing clothes. But at the same time, I feel like I've always had this complicated relationship with friendship, and specifically with female friendship.

Friends have always been terribly important to me. But navigating the friendships themselves has always been fraught. I used to be very confused by this—it didn't make sense that someone who wanted and needed friends as badly as I did would have such a difficult time holding on to them. But therapy and hindsight have illuminated so much in the last few years.

For one, I am not straight, but I didn't realize I was queer until a few years ago. It's made some of my messier friendships make a lot more sense and it's also illuminated some of the recurring conflicts that existed between me and a few of my female friends over the years—there were times when I wanted to be more than friends and didn't know how to manage the romantic feelings alongside the platonic ones.

But perhaps more importantly: For much of my life, I had an overwhelming and deep fear of abandonment. I won't bore you with the psychobabble that informed this breakthrough, but suffice it to say, if and when friends ever became a little distant, I became increasingly clingy. And because I also did not realize my own value, I was always convinced people would leave me.

I had and have friends because I am sweet, funny, kind, and cute; because I'm a great listener. I'm thoughtful and friendly, and when I mess up, I do my best to take responsibility for my actions and to make things right. But none of this seemed valuable to me when I was younger. I could see my friends' infinite worth, because they were, of course, more than worthy. I would be quick to point out the joy a funny friend added to my life, the peace friends who validated my feelings gave me, the exuberance I felt being around friends who were courageous. I just didn't recognize my own worthiness. That the softness my sensitivity brought out in friends with a hard outer shell helped them feel more human, or that my nonjudgmental nature meant so many people thought of me as a safe place—a person they could come to for help or compassion when they had nowhere else to turn. I only saw my shortcomings. I focused on the moments or ways I failed my friends or the gifts others had that I was lacking instead of what was special and unique about me.

This was perhaps because my particular set of gifts aren't ones typically celebrated by our individualistic society. Softness, for example, is seen as weakness by so many that for a long time that was how I saw my ability to be gentle and my quickness to cry, my deep capacity for kindness and my high level of natural empathy. I thought it was bad. I thought it made me less worthy, because I should be stronger, more independent, less affected by the world and mean words or cruelty. I thought it was something I should hide and that if anyone were to discover how deep my sensitivity ran, it would be another reason for them to leave.

Because I didn't recognize my own value, it was easy for me to assume I had nothing to offer. And if I didn't have anything to offer, why would anyone choose to be or stay my friend?

I share all of this just in case you feel this way too—like you don't understand why people like you. If you find that your inner monologue is asking "Why would anyone want to be my friend?" here is your answer: **You're wonderful.** And I mean that literally—*you are full of wonder.* You may not see it yet, or believe it, or know all the ways your particular kind of wonder works, but take it from me . . . There is magic inside you.

We all have it. But it shows up differently in each of us. And I think that in addition to friendship being these shared kindnesses that Michelle mentions, it's also about finding people who have a kind of magic that complements or expands your own.

If you're someone who cries easily like me, maybe your magic is your ability to feel your feelings unguardedly. Do you know how rare that is? How wonderful a gift that could be to show and share with a friend?

Maybe you're someone who sees what they want and goes after it no matter what. You never quit. That kind of ambition can propel you and empower your friends to shoot their shots too.

Say you're quiet. More than likely you're an incredible observer. You're the one who always remembers birthdays and who gives the best advice because you know what makes everyone tick. You know what they need before they name it. Like Stephen Chbosky wrote in *The Perks of Being a Wallflower*: "You see things. You keep quiet about them. And you understand."

If you're the opposite, the loud friend, you might be the life of the party, the joy bringer, the one who celebrates everyone's wins without an ounce of jealousy. This is precious. I don't know what I would do without my friends who have this trait—they are my biggest cheerleaders.

So yes, friendship is about swapping small kindnesses. But it's also about recognizing your own gifts and value, seeing how precious and worthy of love you are. And being willing to share the best parts of you with those you choose, and who choose you back.

SIDE NOTE: ON SELF-LOVE

I've had a fear of loss and losing people for as long as I can remember. It is what I find myself writing about in my novels again and again, and so far I seem to be unable to escape it. Some of the fear I can attribute to my lifelong struggle with anxiety because so many of my triggers were and continue to be wrapped up in the safety and well-being of the people I love most. Some of it stems from that fear of abandonment always ringing like a bell inside my brain—a tinkling reminder of a loss I may not have any control over.

I looked for signs of loss or the possibility of it everywhere. Sometimes I even wonder if my constant fear of losing people was predestined. Because I had a twin.

What I mean when I say I had a twin is that I literally had one. My mother did not know she was pregnant with twins, and I don't know if that failing was due to the times and the technology or if whoever did her first ultrasound just made a mistake. Perhaps, for instance, our heartbeats were synced up during the initial visit so that only one was heard; that happens quite often with twin pregnancies. Whatever the case, my mom was pregnant for just a few weeks before she started bleeding, and when she went to the doctor, she was told that she'd had a miscarriage.

My mother left heartbroken, thinking that

she was no longer pregnant. She was supposed to go back to have a procedure done that would remove any remaining tissue from the pregnancy, but she was so sad that she didn't show up for her follow-up appointment. Again, I don't know if this was a breakdown of the system or the technology, but this procedure is an important one. Women can fall ill without it, so someone should have followed up with her. But no one did.

A few weeks later she noticed she was continuing to put on weight, and when she finally did reschedule her appointment, it was confirmed, to her and her doctor's surprise, that she was still pregnant. That there had been two babies, a follow-up ultrasound revealed, because there were two amniotic sacs. But now one was empty.

I could spend more time on this story, diving into how Black women are statistically more likely to be ignored, neglected, and their pain underestimated by professionals in the medical field. Black moms and babies also die at a much higher rate during labor and delivery than their white counterparts—over 200 percent more frequently, but I digress.

The point is, when I found out when I was seven or eight that I'd had a twin, I thought it made so much sense. I had always been an intensely lonely kid. I'd always felt out of place, like something (or maybe someone!) was missing. And then it turned out someone always had been missing. Having a built-in best friend (the way all twin media in the '90s said twins always were) was very appealing, and though I didn't know the twin's gender, I built an elaborate fantasy around them being a girl. I longed for my twin sister.

Full disclosure: Sometimes I still do.

I also have an older sister who I don't know very well. She's my father's daughter from a previous relationship and we visited her a couple times a year when I was younger, but I haven't spoken to her in years. I always had this enduring fantasy that one day we'd be closer. I still think about that sometimes too.

I think I fixated on my nonexistent twin and my estranged sister in the way that I did for the same reason: I wanted someone who loved and accepted me unconditionally, other than my parents. I wanted to be chosen. And I think what I wanted more than anything was a built-in forever friend—one who couldn't get sick of me and leave.

Wrapped up in that fear of being left was the assumption that I was more leaveable than lovable. Once I learned to love myself, in all my absurd messiness, that fear of people leaving didn't evaporate completely, but the high-pitched, ever-present sound of it became much quieter in my head.

Michelle Obama often writes and speaks about the importance of self-love. One quote of hers about this stands out to me more than the others: "We need to do a better job of putting ourselves higher on our own 'to do' list." I've spent huge parts of my life being overly preoccupied with other people—trying to keep them safe from circumstances I couldn't control, people-pleasing in an attempt to make sure they wanted to stick around, worrying about others constantly and always putting their needs before my own. But learning to prioritize myself, a skill I'll admit I'm still mastering, has made so many of my other concerns melt away. When I'm doing a good job of loving myself (ensuring my self-talk is positive and uplifting or at the very least gentle, showing myself the same compassion I show others whenever I make a mistake, getting enough sleep and even drinking more water), I've found that I'm better able to show up for the people I love. Taking care of and loving myself allows me to better take care of and love others. It seems obvious, but it isn't simple.

So take a step back. If you want to be the best version of yourself—a great friend or an awesome sibling or a thoughtful partner—make sure your needs are met first. You must love yourself and know and believe you're worthy of the love you want others to show you. You can't expect anyone else to see your loveliness if you don't see it (and nurture it) yourself first.

When they go low,

we go high.

—MICHELLE OBAMA,
Democratic National Convention speech, 2016

REMEMBER THE BULLY I TOLD YOU ABOUT from seventh grade? The one who tortured me daily for months? Well, after nearly a year of bullying me and several other people in our grade, she got jumped.

Now, I realize that telling this story might be the opposite of going high, but I'm going to tell it anyway.

Let me set the scene: It was sixth-period geography. It was spring because I remember it being close to the end of the school year, but it couldn't have been June yet because though the classroom was warm, it wasn't so warm we needed to turn on the massive, noisy air-conditioning unit every classroom in the old school building was equipped with.

I know the air conditioner wasn't on because from my seat I wouldn't have been able to hear what was happening closer to the front of the room. That's where the bully was sitting across from one of my friends.

Bully was bullying as usual, but it had been an exceptionally rough day for some reason. Everyone was in a terrible mood. Maybe all the girls in my friend group had our periods or something. I do remember us all being synced up. Whatever it was, tensions were running high and we were all a bit on edge. The whole class also hated the geography teacher, and it was the last class of the day. He was often unable to wrangle us even though my class was on the talented and gifted track. We were supposedly the "smart, good" kids.

Everyone was talking like it was the start of

class—just a complete ruckus, a cacophony of voices—but because it was this teacher, it could have been any point during the forty-five-minute period.

So, Bully says something awful to the friend of mine who she's sitting next to. I don't remember what it was, but I do remember hearing it and thinking, *Oh shit*. And I guess my friend was tired of taking the crap she and the rest of us had been taking all that day, week, and year. She snapped, and I only knew she'd snapped because she very calmly removed her hijab. This particular friend only removed her hijab right before she threw a punch, because as she told me once, "I don't want to give whoever I'm fighting the satisfaction." (Yes, she was a badass.)

So she took off her hijab, and Bully clearly

didn't know that meant something bad was coming her way, because the next thing I remember is them both being on the floor, desks knocked sideways, and all the students in sixth-period geography screaming. Then my other friend jumped in, and a third followed closely behind, yelling something like, "Oh hell no you don't." I, however, did not jump in. I stood by silently, horrified and in tears.

I would love to say that I didn't join in on the bully beatdown because I thought it was inherently wrong. But to be completely honest, I don't know if that's true. I think I thought it was karma. Cosmic retribution. She'd been so awful for so long (a "piece of work," in my mother's words) that, in a just world, she had something like this coming to her. But I think I did know that I didn't want to hurt her just because she had hurt me. Somewhere deep inside, I think I knew she must already be hurting. In that moment, I went high.

Michelle Obama has said that bullies are scared people hiding inside scary people, that we should go high when they go low, and that we should ignore the haters. And I take comfort in the fact that she did just that throughout her time in the White House and for all the years she's been in the public eye both before and after Barack Obama's presidency. I also think she's right. I know jumping into that fight would not have made me feel better. I think I knew it then too.

In the end, I was still suspended because my school wanted to "teach me a lesson." These were the people I was hanging out with, after all, they told me, and even though I wasn't fighting, I needed to learn what happened when you had the wrong kinds of friends.

I'll pause here briefly to mention how much more frequently Black boys and girls are suspended than their white counterparts for equivalent or lesser offenses, but I won't go too deep. You can google it if you care to.

My mother, God love her, raised hell about them punishing me for something I hadn't done, threatened to go to the superintendent to place a complaint, and promised to encourage the other involved parents to look into exactly what had happened in that geography class. Unlike me, my mother, admittedly, did not go high. The administration rescinded my suspension and said I could come back to school the very next day, but by then my mother was too angry to accept, probably because of how upset I had been by the whole event and after learning the bully had been given a shorter suspension than everyone else because she "hadn't started it." As a result, my mom let me ride out my bogus suspension at home, where she said I deserved some downtime for dealing with Bully for so long. For those three days, she let me do whatever I want.

After our suspensions were over, the bully was a lot more mild mannered. She even tried to be my friend. Much like how Michelle and Barack are always courteous to the news organizations, other politicians, and pundits who have been disrespectful to them, I'm pleased to report that I was always kind to her, though I never hung out

with her again. Instead I found new friends—
girls I still know and love and talk to weekly, even
now.

I know it was only the comeuppance of a
middle school mean girl, but I'm still proud of
little me. I think Michelle would have been too.

If there's one thing
I've learned in life,
it's the power of
using your voice.

—MICHELLE OBAMA,
Becoming

THIS QUOTE REMINDS ME A LOT OF THAT moment in Spider-Man when someone says to Peter, "With great power comes great responsibility." I'm not a big comics fan, but that line has always stuck with me. Because we're all infinitely powerful, though it takes most of us years to realize it. And our voices are one of the biggest sources of that strength.

From a very young age, I knew that my voice had power. I credit my mother for instilling this belief in me at the very beginning of my life. As far back as I can remember—maybe since the first grade—she let me drag her away from the rest of the family daily so I could speak to her "in private," and I unloaded every detail of my days into her listening ears. She asked me lots of questions to keep up with all my elementary and middle and high school dramas and shared in my triumphs and failures. I told her nearly everything and she kept every one of my secrets, and that made me confident that what I had to say mattered in a way that I don't think anything else would have. Because my mother listened to me, I knew that people, regardless of who they were, deserved to be listened to. I knew that my thoughts and feelings were important. And I knew that what I had to say was unique and different from what anyone else on Earth could contribute. But knowing that your voice has power, and understanding the best ways to use that power, are two totally different things.

As a teen, I was quick to talk back. I think the angst of tweendom and early teenhood hit me hard, right in the gut. And because I knew my own power, I began to resent all the adults around me for no reason other than the fact that they all had a different kind of power—one that was inherently theirs because they were older than me and one that they constantly exerted over me. I developed a bit of an issue with authority out of nowhere, and if an adult (who wasn't my mother or father) was saying something I didn't want to hear, I didn't listen. I also often, for lack of a better term, popped off.

This power struggle was constant. It sometimes happened with people at my church. "Sisters" and "brothers" who took to heart the saying that it takes a village to raise a child often found that I wasn't a child who wanted to be raised by anyone in the village other than her own parents.

I got into trouble all the time for saying something along those lines ("Well, I'll ask my mother what she thinks about that" or "Did my father ask you to tell me this?") to church members who sought to correct or address my behavior, a low-key "Don't come for me unless I ask for you" that I delivered with the IDGAF attitude of someone much older than I was.

It happened with family members. Uncles who had opinions about my friends or boyfriends and older cousins who wanted to save me from neighborhood kids who they thought were a bad influence were often ignored or dismissed.

I spoke back to my teachers so much that I had detention almost every day of seventh *and* eighth grade. I loudly accused them of sexism if I thought they treated male and female students differently; talked over my classmates if I thought they were wrong; rebuffed hall monitors who tried to rush me to or from the bathroom. I had to stay after school so often that my Uncle Boo nicknamed me "D.T." So using my voice was never something I had to learn.

What I did have to figure out, though, was *when* to use my voice; *how* to harness the power I already knew I had and use it to my advantage, or for the benefit of others. And that took years.

I of course use my voice all the time now. As a writer, it's literally my job. And I try my hardest to make sure I'm creating stories and books that bring light into the world, that reflect the best and worst parts of being human back to us without judgment or contempt. My hope is that my voice will always be a positive force in the universe; that

I will make this place and the people I encounter feel a little better than they did before.

Perhaps Michelle Obama knew the power of her own voice before she started on the presidential campaign trail with her husband, but if she didn't, that was the place where her power and influence became clear. While Barack focused on swing states, bringing minority voters to the polls, and reeling in those under thirty-five with his moving speeches, Michelle worked her magic on just about everyone else. Using her trademark realness, occasional sarcasm, and wit, Michelle spoke authentically about how little she enjoyed politics, but was vocal and firm about where she (and her husband) stood on the issues. She told stories about her humble beginnings and growing up in a blue-collar family, which endeared her to the working class, and when she spoke about her Ivy League education and professional career, she appealed to coastal elites. She earned the nickname "The Closer" because she so often persuaded undecided voters to sign pledge cards in Barack's favor.

So Michelle is right. There is great power in using your voice. Everything you say (or write!) matters and can have a lasting effect on both your own world and the lives of those around you. You are infinitely powerful, remember? And "with great power comes great responsibility," so you must learn to recognize and believe in your own power. You must learn when and how to use it. Otherwise, you may cause damage where you don't mean to. Otherwise, you may end up a villain in your own story.

Don't ever underestimate the importance you can have, because history has shown us that courage can be contagious, and hope can take on a life of its own.

—MICHELLE OBAMA,
Young African Women
Leaders Forum, 2011

I'VE ALWAYS BEEN A WORRIER.

I used to call my mother repeatedly if she was working late, convinced something awful had happened to her. I sobbed if I missed the due date for an essay, and I could spend hours panicking about school assignments I didn't understand. I was preoccupied by constant and vivid intrusive thoughts of random terrible things happening to me or my loved ones, and I never understood why I felt nervous and sweaty at grocery stores or in crowds. There were nights I couldn't sleep because I'd convince myself that the rhythm of my own pulse was the sound of intruders walking around on the floor below in combat boots. (I *know*.) Turns out I wasn't just "a worrier." I was experiencing all these things because I have anxiety.

I didn't know that I had anxiety, which is a diagnosable chemical imbalance in the brain that affects close to 18 percent of people in the United States, until I was in my thirties. I didn't know that anxiety has mental and emotional symptoms like insomnia, nervousness, sensory overload, and constant worry or fear (things I'd accepted as a normal part of my existence) until I was an adult. It can also cause physical symptoms, including but not limited to chest pain, increased heart rate, excessive sweating, or chills. It can cause nausea or diarrhea, hyperventilation, and the inability to focus. It can make you cry. Anxiety can make you feel completely powerless against the onslaught of the world and the symptoms can make you feel like you've lost control of your own brain and body. It can be terrifying. It is a cruel illness that can make you feel hopeless and completely useless at once. But I'm getting ahead of (and a little down on) myself. Let me rewind a bit.

I went to a very nerdy and incredibly competitive high school. It is a public magnet school, which means it attracts the "smartest," most ambitious kids from all over Washington, DC, to apply and attend. It was and is branded so aggressively as college preparatory that the administration practically guarantees that the kids who go there will get into any college of their choice. As a result, the school was hopelessly and completely focused on academics.

In addition to being one of the first public schools in DC to offer the International Baccalaureate (or IB) program, my high school offered more AP classes than almost every other high school in the city, a staggering number of my classmates took classes at nearby universities, and it lived up to the hype: Nearly 100 percent of students from my class graduated and went on to college, many starting as second-semester freshmen because of the college credits they'd already racked up. There were clubs and student government, but there weren't any varsity sports. Privately donated funds were usually allocated to things like new books, the state-of-the-art science lab, or updated computers. And at the end of every quarter, the top ten GPAs from every grade were posted in the hallway in front of the auditorium, with the students' names and rankings like a sports roster or castings for a school musical.

I will never forget how, during the tour prior

to enrolling, they told parents to expect their kids to have three to four hours of homework every single night of the week, and that we'd get early dismissal on Wednesdays to complete the community service hours required to graduate—nearly three times what was required to graduate from any other public school in the District. For someone like me, who was a perfectionist and already riddled with anxiety, it was brutal.

At the time, though, I didn't even know what anxiety was. I didn't understand that my constant fear of failure, my difficulty sleeping, my panic attacks and feelings of hopelessness were connected. They were the result of how I was hardwired and would soon be exacerbated by high school, which proved to be a very stressful environment. But I didn't figure that out until years later.

Michelle Obama attended a highly competitive college preparatory school too. Whitney M. Young Magnet High School opened its doors in 1975, and only two years later the future First Lady would pass the required tests to enroll. The school sits on a quiet corner in Chicago's Near West Side neighborhood, straddling the line between the North and South Sides, and was a collection of new, modern buildings, connected by a glass skyway that awed Michelle the first time she saw it. It was named after Whitney Moore Young Jr., an African American civil rights leader who worked to end employment discrimination, and it opened with the goal that its student population would reflect the vibrantly diverse population of the city of Chicago, but it took a while before the school achieved this goal—the organic integration that was hoped for wasn't easy to attain. At the time of Michelle's enrollment, more than 80 percent of the students were non-white, at least in part because parents of white children preferred the private institutions in the city over public ones. And, Michelle suspected, because white parents weren't comfortable with how many kids of color were in attendance at Whitney Young.

The school was only twelve miles from the house Michelle and her family lived in on the South Side, but it felt worlds away. Every morning at five a.m. for all four years of high school, Michelle would take two city buses to school, transferring to a second route to complete the journey across Chicago. She shared her commute with young professionals and families, and as the bus passed through downtown, she admired the shiny, tall buildings, not knowing that she'd one day work in them. The daily commute took more than an hour, and as she rode from one side of the city to the other, she couldn't help but notice how the people changed too: from poor and working-class to rich, from mostly brown and Black to white.

Initially, she worried she wouldn't measure up to her new classmates. High school was the first time she encountered a population of Black elite—Black kids whose parents had white-collar jobs and who lived in sprawling, affluent neighborhoods. There were kids like her there too, of course, Black kids from the South Side and other less-wealthy parts of the city, but with everything she did at school both in and outside the classroom, she felt she was representing her neighborhood and every Black girl from the South Side. She worried that if she didn't excel, it might reinforce stereotypes she knew the wealthier students held about people from where she lived—or worse, that if she did excel, she might be seen as inauthentic by other South Side kids.

Similar to the pressure Michelle felt at Whitney Young, everything about my experience as a high school student was triggering: the huge amounts of homework, the expectations of attending not only college but preferably an Ivy League one, the GPA posting, and the hypervigilance on the parts of the teachers and staff when it came to the students' behavior. The school was so tiny, there was nowhere to hide, no possibility of fading into the background. I also worried about representing my family, neighborhood, and race well—it was impossible not to.

In the four years that I was a student there, I had countless panic attacks. I had intrusive thoughts that kept me up at night even after I'd studied for hours. I knew students who were going gray early from the stress and still others who were straight-up *losing* their hair. Some kids had rashes and developed ulcers—and all of it, from the panic to the hair problems, was happening because we were all stressed the hell out. At one point I got an unexplained rash on my upper arm. It was itchy and red and it would flare up and go away at seemingly random times. The doctor gave me a steroid cream to treat it and said it was from "stress," and I'd completely forgotten about it until the same thing happened to me again at the beginning of the pandemic. The brain can do strange things to the body when it's under tremendous stress. But "stress," it seems, was an early-90s euphemism for anxiety.

Somehow in the midst of it all, my friends and I still found small ways to enjoy high school. We influenced and changed so many things that had, until us, been accepted as hard-and-fast rules. I wish I could say we overhauled the community service program so that it required a more realistic time commitment or that we protested the hours-long reading assignments. We didn't. But we *did* run for and win the election to be the heads of student government. We planned and executed several off-campus school-sponsored parties because we were tired of teacher-organized dances no one came to in the gym. We organized community and school cleanups and supported each other when teachers or classes got to be too much. We got into trouble for bringing a stereo to lunch to celebrate one of our birthdays, but then other students started doing it too, which really helped boost morale and liven up the place. Our courage, you could say, was contagious. We made the best of a very hostile, stressful place for ourselves and our fellow classmates while we could. And my friends from high school and I remain very close, even now.

Michelle's insecurities about school were quickly assuaged—she discovered that everyone there had a similar goal in mind: college. Here was a place where it was okay to be smart, so she felt safe to embrace what had always come naturally to her.

Michelle made the honor roll her first semester, and her hard work and stellar grades kept her there all four years. She danced before and after classes in the school's gorgeous arts building, and was also a member of the National Honor Society, student council, and would go on to graduate the salutatorian of her class.

When the time came to apply to college, Michelle set her sights high. Her brother had been accepted to Princeton two years earlier, and Michelle knew shortly after a visit to the campus that she wanted to follow in his footsteps. Unfortunately, a guidance counselor thought Princeton was out of reach for a girl like her, perhaps because she was Black, perhaps because she was from the South Side, or maybe it was a little of both.

Michelle has told this story dozens of times. How the counselor spoke down to her, how it made her feel small but also determined to prove the woman wrong. "They told me I was never going to get into a school like Princeton. I still hear that doubt ringing in my head," she said. But "they" were wrong.

But why am I talking about my bonkers high school and my ongoing struggle with anxiety? And Michelle Obama's high school years too? I think the heart of Michelle Obama's message in the quote at the start of this chapter is this: Don't underestimate yourself. You can do incredible work and great things regardless of where you start or where you are. Michelle talks constantly of her humble beginnings, but they launched her into the world with everything she needed to become the giant she is now. People underestimating her just gave her fuel to prove them wrong. Her courage is certainly contagious, and both she and Barack remain a source of hope for people everywhere.

There was a time when an off-campus dance seemed impossible at my school. But we made it happen largely on our own despite very little support from the administration. I may have felt completely overwhelmed most days by my academic workload, but I made it through and came out on the other side. My friends and I gave each other hope in big and small ways, so that even on our darkest days we were able to show up and work toward something that so often felt unattainable: getting out of high school.

But here we are on the other side. We made it. Michelle made it.

You will make it too.

As someone who coped with anxiety for a very long time without knowing or even understanding what was happening in my brain and body, there are a few things I wish I'd known sooner. So just in case this is happening to you or someone you love, I want to say those things here.

Your pain is real. I won't lie—I'm dramatic. I always have been. I can become extremely excited about the smallest things. I rejoice, loudly, at the successes of my friends, and I've been known to squeal when I see a cute baby or dog. I laugh without reservation at funny jokes and movies, and I sometimes bounce in my seat at restaurants when I spot my food coming out of the kitchen. Because of my natural tendency toward histrionics, there have been times when I'd been having a panic attack or been in the throes of an anxiety-induced migraine or when I'd become completely overwhelmed in a grocery store or crowd and my pain in those moments was ignored. "Oh, please. You're fine" is something I heard quite often from friends or relatives who didn't understand. The truth was, my pain was and is real, no matter how dramatic I am on other occasions. Yours is too.

You deserve compassion, from others and from yourself. In moments when you might feel panicky or overwhelmed, like you can't breathe or your world is coming to an end, you deserve softness. You deserve to be treated with care, to be listened to, to be validated. No one knows what it's like to be you in any given moment except *you*. You are an expert on yourself and that expertise should be respected. Lean into the people (whether they're family members, friends, mental-health-care professionals, or others) who prove again and again that they can be a soft place for you to land. Those people are invaluable to your past, present, and future healing. And while those outside sources of compassion are extremely important, don't forget to be gentle to and within yourself too. A trick from therapy that has helped me transform my negative self-talk and find an internal gentleness for myself was to find a photo of me at a very young age, maybe from when I was four or five, and now I always imagine I'm speaking to that version of myself, especially in moments when my anxiety is exceptionally high. If it's difficult for you to imagine a younger version of yourself, I've also found some success with imagining a small person I love.

If you have a younger brother or sister, cousin, niece or nephew—anyone who is very young but whom you love very much and feel fiercely protective of—imagine you're speaking to that person when you're having not-so-great thoughts and feelings about yourself or when you're feeling anxious. Might that tiny adjustment help you be kinder to you?

You are not crazy. Your feelings are always valid, but I know I'm not alone in being made to feel that they aren't. At times when I've voiced concerns about things that weren't a big deal to someone else, I was often made to feel as if I were being completely irrational. Over time, this caused me to question almost all my feelings. I would be deeply hurt by something someone said, or I'd be feeling overstimulated in an everyday situation, and instead of listening to my heart and body, I would interrogate myself, trying to figure out if what I was thinking and feeling was "right." That constant questioning eventually made me feel like I couldn't trust myself, and that, my friends, is a very dangerous place to be. When you don't trust that your interpretation of the world is real and valid, it makes it harder to stand up for yourself and more difficult to understand the world around you. Know this: If you feel something, that feeling is real, but I want to be clear that a feeling is not an excuse for bad behavior. The real magic happens when you do the work and begin to understand why certain people or situations make you feel the way you do. Once you begin to understand the reasons and experiences that guide and influence your feelings, you'll be unstoppable.

You are limitless. Anxiety has a way of making you feel powerless, when the opposite is true. People with anxiety tend to be more empathetic than the average human, which makes us more sensitive, compassionate, and accepting in friendships and romantic relationships. We tend to be some of the most effective leaders because we're able to see and anticipate multiple outcomes and because we're more careful in our decision-making. We have a built-in security system—a kind of sixth sense that allows us to feel, in our guts, when something is wrong. And even if we ignore all these specific qualities, it is still true. Everyone has the ability to hone their power. You just have to come to understand when your anxiety is speaking, and when you should and shouldn't listen.

Good relationships feel good.
They feel right. They don't hurt.

—MICHELLE OBAMA,
address to Elizabeth Garrett
Anderson students, 2011

WHEN I WAS SEVENTEEN, I DATED A GUY
who was twenty-two. Yes, I know. It wasn't the greatest choice, and he wasn't the greatest guy, but at the time, that wasn't something I could see clearly.

I was a senior, excited about the possibility of what life after high school might look like, and here was this guy who was already living that life: He was out of school and on his own, doing all the things that felt just out of my reach. But there was always something a little dark about him; a negative energy I couldn't ever quite articulate. He was almost like a cloud, casting a shadow over everything.

But there was also something exciting about him . . . something a tiny bit dangerous. I don't think I ever introduced him to my parents, though they knew I was seeing someone "older," and the fact that I didn't want to introduce him should have been a sign. There were so many signs, to be honest, that this wasn't it. But I brushed right past them, thrilled to embark on this new thing—to be wanted by someone who, to be frank, shouldn't have wanted me.

Most of the time, the relationship felt fine. He took me out, he paid for everything we did together, and though he talked about himself a lot, rarely leaving much space for me and my thoughts in the conversations we had (another sign), he was affectionate and mostly nice to me. Still, the relationship never felt completely good or even very "right." You know the warm feeling you get in your gut when you really like someone and they like you back? When it feels like stepping into a beam of sunlight every time you see them? I never felt that way with him.

There were also moments, usually when we were alone in the car, when things got a little darker; when our relationship went from feeling mostly okay to definitively wrong. I won't mince words here: Whenever we hooked up, things almost always went further than I wanted them to. He invited me over to his place often, but I always refused to go, suggesting that we meet at the mall or the movies or a restaurant instead. Though I liked the idea of him having his own apartment (that was a part of his "older guy" appeal), I knew if he crossed my boundaries in a car, I'd have absolutely no control over what happened in a space where we'd be utterly alone. I rarely overtly said no to his advances, but I also almost never said yes.

At the time I assumed that if I didn't try to stop him, and if things weren't violent, anything that happened between us was fine. I know now that he was assaulting me. I know now that yes means yes and that everything else means no. I know now that it wasn't my fault.

But for a long time I rationalized his behavior, and my own reactions. I don't blame myself for doing this because we live in a world where victims of sexual violence are often the ones who are questioned, instead of the perpetrators. I asked myself all the questions I thought others would ask me, knowing in my gut that something was wrong: *Did you say no? Did he force himself on you? Well, isn't he your boyfriend?* And all my answers made me feel . . . I don't know. Like I was being dramatic. Like my gut was wrong. Maybe I felt a little bit empty too. A little bit like I was all alone.

None of the answers to these questions matter, of course. They don't make me complicit because consent isn't complicated. And anyway, those are the wrong questions. I should have been asking myself if I felt safe. If I felt comfortable. If I wanted everything that was happening to be happening. If it felt good.

It didn't feel good. It didn't feel right. And I knew I was uncomfortable being alone with him. Luckily, when I started college, it was easy enough to break things off—we both knew there was nothing between us to try and save once there were a few hundred miles between us instead.

Take it from me: If you're uncomfortable

being alone with anyone, that means *something*. A gut feeling is valid and enough. Don't let anyone, including your own brain, talk you out of that.

The guy I'd dated before the twenty-two-year-old was the first guy I'd loved. He was quiet, kind, and considerate. He was gentle and thoughtful and he treated me like a queen. I dated him for almost two years, breaking up briefly and getting back together when he accompanied me to a dance despite us being "on a break" and whispered this into my ear during a slow dance, like we were on the set of a movie: "You know I still want you, right?"

Everything about and with him felt good: The way he held my hand. The way he planned things for us to do. The way he always waited for me to make the first move or to definitively say yes before he took things any further. He constantly checked on me, called me, asked me questions. He knew me well and was always trying to get to know me better. He felt like the sun.

When Michelle first met Barack, she had heard about him for weeks leading up to his arrival. She'd heard people uttering his unusual name and coworkers saying that he was from Hawaii. She'd learned that he was only a first-year law student but that her firm had decided to take him on as an associate anyway, a rare and impressive feat. A few lawyers Michelle worked with who'd interacted with him during his interview mentioned that he was brilliant, and a few others even said he was cute.

After all the anticipation, his first day was a bit disappointing. It was raining and he showed up late and wet, and Michelle began to wonder if the hype that preceded him was just that—hype. She figured her white associates wouldn't have very high standards when it came to a Black guy; just the fact that he was at Harvard would probably be enough to surpass the expectations most of them had, whether they were willing to admit it or not.

Michelle, on the other hand, was much harder to impress. But after she got over his somewhat lackluster first impression, she was struck by how sure of himself he seemed—that confidence Barack's granddad had hoped he'd inherit from his father had somehow found its way to him. Michelle had gone from her tough magnet high school to Princeton to Harvard to her job at Sidley Austin—a straight shot from one decision to the next full of hard work and meant to produce success through a proven and some would say formulaic strategy. He was more of a wanderer, and though his path was more indirect than hers had been, she could see that he was sure that the decisions he'd made (transferring halfway through undergrad, working as a community organizer before moving forward with law school) were right for him despite his untraditional trajectory. That intrigued her. In spite of her initial apprehension, she quickly grew fond of him.

Barack, on the other hand, was immediately taken with Michelle. He's since said that he was instantly struck by how tall and beautiful she was, and that having her assigned as his mentor was the luckiest break of his life.

They grew closer over the course of their first month working together. Barack would ask her out dozens of times before she'd eventually agree, adamantly refusing because she felt it was inappropriate, tacky, and not what he'd come to the firm to do. She didn't relent until he offered to leave his position if that's what it took to date her, insisting that her concerns about appearances were unfounded. So she finally said yes because something about him just felt right.

Follow your gut. Go with what feels right. And always, always seek out the light.

One of the most useless questions an adult can ask a child—*What do you want to be when you grow up?* As if growing up is finite.

—MICHELLE OBAMA,
Becoming

WHEN I WAS THIRTY, MARRIED TO THE MAN
of my dreams, a few years into my career as a marketing professional, and shortly after selling my first novel, I came out as queer to my husband. I remember staring at these dried flowers from our wedding as I told him, thinking about how they'd bloomed and how they'd be exactly as they were now, forever. I remember wishing I could be that way—frozen at my most beautiful, instead of being this finicky, always changing, sometimes ugly (and always confusing) human thing. It was not graceful or neat, my confession. I cried a lot. We had a bumpy couple of months, but we made it to the other side.

I start this essay in this way because we are conditioned to believe that by the time we are of a certain age or in a certain place in our careers or once our personal lives reach or pass particular milestones, we are in some way "complete." Making the opposite also true, right? That if we haven't done certain things by a certain age, we're incomplete. Both these things are dead wrong. And I have a theory that it all starts with asking kids this pointless question.

As a kid, Michelle and her parents spoke often about the kind of future she wanted for herself. Inspired by her own mother's diligence when it came to her and her brother, she'd imagined becoming a mother from a very young age, but as she matured, so did her ambitions. She dreamed of possibilities like becoming a doctor or a lawyer, and community outreach found its way into her future goals too, partially because of her father's involvement as a Democratic precinct captain (someone who went door-to-door making sure constituents were registered to vote, answering questions about the candidates, the political process, and more), and partially because Michelle knew she wanted to do work that helped people. Her parents encouraged their daughter to continue to dream and made sure she had every opportunity they could afford. And even a few they couldn't.

As Michelle grew older, she noticed changes in and around her neighborhood because of redlining, which is a discriminatory practice that was popular during the 1960s and 1970s to keep cities segregated. Her elementary school had been large, crowded, and almost exclusively Black, but Chicago as a whole was beginning to take small steps toward integration. And as she traveled in and out of her neighborhood, for school and extracurricular involvement, Michelle had to learn how to straddle two worlds: the one where she was a girl from the South Side, and the one where she was a girl who wanted *more*.

This led to Michelle questioning her identity—she wanted to be genuinely herself, unashamed of where she came from, while also not hiding her desire for success. And it wasn't always easy straddling that line. It often put her at odds with friends and family members who assumed she thought she was better than they were. But luckily, her parents were there to reassure her that who she was and what she wanted was valid, and that her identities weren't mutually exclusive— that she could be both brilliant and Black.

She grew up to hold a variety of jobs, but it was the ones in public service that she felt exemplified who she'd always thought she was—who she'd always wanted to be. But even now, Michelle will admit that she isn't done growing, that she is still herself *becoming*.

I wasn't like Michelle. For the longest time, I didn't know what I wanted to be when I grew up. But even though that uncertainty was completely normal and true, "I don't know" was never, ever what I said. I was always trying to be Little Miss Perfect, remember? I was always trying to be whatever people expected me to be. Always seeking external validation. I was constantly working super hard to not be seen as a failure. And saying "I don't know" to the "What do you want to be when you grow up?" question felt like a fundamental failure of childhood. To not have a goal or even a wish for my future felt wrong. So I began doing something dangerous: I began to say I wanted to be whatever other people said I should be.

For a while, I told everyone who asked me that question that I wanted to be an architect. One day my dad suggested it out of the blue. "You like to draw," I remember him saying while he towered over little me, where I sat sketching something on computer paper I'd stolen from the cracked printer tray. "And you're great at math," he said, adding things up, it seemed, in that moment in his own head. I was okay at math. I knew my times tables a little early, but that was just memorization. And I mostly learned it early because of the wanting to be perfect thing. So was I good at math? I'm not exactly sure. But he seemed sure. He seemed super confident that being an architect was the perfect thing for me to want to be when I grew up. And I latched on to it, though that day was the first time I'd even heard the word. I had no idea what it meant, so I asked. "Oh. Well, it's someone who designs buildings. Don't worry, you'll get to draw and use math."

"Oh, okay," I imagine I must have said. My father had always regretted not finishing his engineering degree, so I think this was also a part of the logic behind his suggestion. I liked that it wasn't one of the typical answers, like doctor, lawyer, or vet. It wasn't childish sounding either, like the way I thought of the kids who wanted to be astronauts because they liked space, or ballerinas because they liked wearing tutus. It was unique. It felt sophisticated. After test running it on a few adults, I *loved* that they all seemed impressed when I gave it as an answer. So for years an architect was what I "wanted" to be.

I am not being as generous as I should be about my father. I *was* very creative and I *did* love making things. I was always working on one project or another—for a long while, I was absolutely obsessed with dioramas, for example. So maybe that was something my father recognized in me too: a love of all things pretty. A passion for aesthetics and art and building beautiful things from scratch. In this he was right.

Then, for a while, I "wanted" to be a model. I shot up to 5'5" before I finished middle school, so everyone just knew I was going to be 5'9" or 5'10" by the time I was done growing. "You're so tall!" people said. "You could be a model." They also told me I should play basketball and I did, terribly, for one harrowing year in the sixth grade. I was never delusional enough to say I wanted to play ball professionally when I grew up, despite everyone's enthusiasm about my height, thank God.

Spoiler alert: I stalled out at 5'7", which is taller than average but definitely not model tall, and anyway, after doing a few fashion shows and going to a couple of auditions, I realized it just wasn't my thing. But modeling, like architecture and basketball, was another hypothetical future of mine that was someone else's idea.

Next was when I wanted to be a fashion designer. This was probably the first thing that was purely my idea. I still loved to draw, and I've always loved clothes, so, logically, there came the day when I started drawing clothes. It was fun, and I think in all honesty, fashion design is a profession I would enjoy. But alas, there was still something that didn't quite click.

All the while, I'd been writing. I journaled my whole life; wrote poetry and short stories and longer pieces that were not quite novellas, but that could have become novels if I'd kept at them. But I never thought writer was an answer I could have to the "What do you want to be?" question. Either that or writing was something I wanted so deeply and badly that I unconsciously didn't dare speak it aloud for fear of jinxing it.

And then shit got real, because I still had no clue what I wanted to be (or who I even was) and the question was about to change.

"What are you majoring in?" became the new refrain, though it was a question that begged for the same kind of answer. *Tell me who you are*, both these questions seem to demand. But, I began to wonder, was that really what the questions sought to uncover?

It was only once I'd gotten to college and started thinking about majors and how people reacted based on my answer that I realized what these questions had been about all along: We like to know what people do, what people want to do, who people are, because we want to assign a certain value to them. *Tell me how I can categorize you in my brain* is what everyone was really asking. *Tell me what I should think of you; if you're worth my time; if you should matter to me at all.*

Sexuality, too, is a thing our society uses to

validate or invalidate individuals' existences. Because of a combination of various factors including, but not limited to, the pervasiveness of the patriarchy, white supremacy, and capitalism in Western culture, when we meet someone, we immediately need to slot them into place, like our brains are . . . vertical filing cabinets or something, and humans are folders. We try to use labels like race, gender identity, sexual orientation, and profession to put people into the proper places in our brain cabinet. For too many people, the closer a human is to a rich cis white hetero male, the higher in the cabinet they get filed.

But back to me. I eventually figured out my major. Often, people rolled their eyes when I told them I was majoring in English, asked if I wanted to be a professor, and when I said no, they told me I'd never make any money. I'm sure that for a while I existed in a low drawer in a lot of people's brain cabinets, but I was okay with that because I knew I was finally moving toward something that was solely based on what I thought and how I felt, instead of what I'd been told to do or be.

I graduated, still a bit unsure, but I knew I was leaning in a direction that felt right. Books felt right. New York felt right. So, despite being told that I should do something else, I learned to trust myself. I learned to lean into what I wanted. I finally went with my gut and waited for the rest to fall into place.

And it did, mostly. I found a great job working with books, and I started writing my own. Until there I was, at thirty, completely sure of what I wanted to be and no longer afraid to say it: a writer. And then, just when I was sure about my career, I realized I had bigger questions about myself to answer.

I'd always liked girls. I've had several friend-ships with blurry boundaries where my feelings crossed the line into the romantic, though I rarely admitted it as it was happening. I was excellent at ignoring things that felt complicated or con-fusing; things that made me question my slowly cracking veneer of perfection. I pushed feelings down or away, pushed friends who were a little more than friends out of my life, and believed that I needed to be what everyone else thought I should be even when it came to this. Just like I'd adopted architect or model as my own aspira-tions, just as I'd played basketball for a year even though I hated sports, I let other people decide this for me too. I was a good, churchgoing girl. So by default, I was straight.

But dear reader, I wasn't. I'm not. I never have been. And the signs were everywhere. It dawned on me that my yearslong admiration of an actress or a singer was not because I wanted to be her, but because I could imagine being with her (what I like to call the "#LifeGoals or #WifeGoals Conundrum"). My voracious consumption of sapphic books and movies and TV shows. The looking back at interactions I've had over the years, recounting them (often in therapy) with the new knowledge of my queerness and having moments again and again where I find myself saying, "Ohhhhh. I did that because I'm kinda gay." And of course the friends I'd loved in messy, complicated ways. Just as I'd finally decided *what*

I wanted to be, I was forced to answer another question: *Who* had I been all along?

I figured that out too, eventually. I had always been a writer. I had always been queer, though I was only finding the name for the feelings I'd always felt thirty years into my existence. And the biggest answer I've found to date? The one Michelle Obama so elegantly stated in the quotation that precedes this essay: We never stop growing, changing, or becoming. It is this concept that gave her the title of her memoir.

Michelle has said in numerous interviews that every decade of her life has brought surprises that she couldn't have imagined in the years before. She credits her openness to possibility— to becoming something and someone she may not have expected—as the main reason she's had such an extraordinary life. What we can learn from her, and perhaps what you can learn from me, is this: Remain open to possibilities. Never stop growing. Make room and space to spend time with yourself, because you are endlessly interesting and there's always more to discover.

I look at the flowers from my wedding differently now. They aren't frozen at their most beautiful—they're stagnant. They're stuck. One day I touched them a little too roughly and petals fell away, littering my floor like confetti. I don't know about you, but I don't want to crumble if things come at me unexpectedly. I want to be like the flowers in a field, alive and wild, changing with the seasons of my life the same way they change with the weather. I want to be like Michelle. Maybe wilting sometimes, but always blossoming again when the time is right.

It's completely normal to not know who you are or what you want to be, because we are all so many different things at once, and we aren't ever done blooming.

Don't ever make
decisions based on fear.
Make decisions based on
hope and possibility.

—MICHELLE OBAMA,
campaign trail in Phoenix, 2008

FAR TOO OFTEN IN SPRING WHEN I SHOULD be looking up at the gorgeous blooming trees, singing birds, and blossoming flowers, I find myself looking down. Before I got a dog, I never noticed. But once I had one, it was impossible to ignore.

I see tiny pink featherless baby birds almost every morning in spring. One or two every day. All on the pavement. All motionless. All as silent as stone. My dog sniffs them out. It may be the ancient predatory wildness left over in her genetics sensing food. But she doesn't eat them, just hesitates long enough for me to notice, look down, yank her away. Just long enough for me to see. For my heart to break a little more as the body count grows.

What is it that drives these tiny featherless

creatures from the safety of their nests? I think there must be something in them that is desperate to see what else is out there, to explore, to fly despite the inherent danger (though maybe they are too young to even realize that the world is dangerous). It could be that staying in the nest is even more unsafe—forgive the pun, but much like sitting ducks, they are just . . . sitting. Or maybe it's hunger that drives them. Thirst. An ignorance to the fact that their mother will return soon with sustenance—that to nourish them and help them thrive is the only reason she'd ever leave them alone.

When I think about fear and choice and the way the two are connected, I think a lot about baby birds. Baby turtles too. Any animal, really, that is born and has a drive to survive that overrides everything else.

For most of us, survival is an evolutionary gift. We're born with the promise that predators won't come knocking on our door or chase us down the sidewalk. But, like birds, our bodies and brains don't realize that. We're still largely ruled by deeply rooted instincts that drive us to protect ourselves from harm. We're hardwired to fear. This charge to make choices and not base them on fear, while wise, is not easy. Fear is ingrained in us to keep us safe. Bucking against that is something I've struggled with my whole life.

I have noticed a pattern, though. All my regrets have their roots in fear-based choices. Similarly, all my greatest accomplishments, the things I'm most proud of, were some of the scariest things I've ever done.

I didn't do study abroad in college because I was terrified about what I would miss out on back at school. Would my friends have new inside jokes I wouldn't understand if I spent a semester in Paris? Would my boyfriend fall for some other girl while I was eating pasta in Rome? Would I meet someone in London and ruin what I already had back home? In the end, the boyfriend I was so worried about losing time with applied for a co-op program that required him to take a se-mester off to work full-time. I didn't even see him much the year I would have been away. I could have been in Sydney, but I was still in Jersey, and even now I wish I had stepped out on faith and taken the leap.

I didn't move to San Francisco. When my boyfriend was offered his dream job clear across the country, I didn't go with him. And while I told anyone who asked that I didn't want to go because of my new job in New York, really I didn't go because I was afraid. What if we moved out there and I couldn't find work? What if we broke up and then I was stranded in this city where I knew no one? What if I loved it there, and decided I wanted to stay even though it was a six-hour flight from my whole family? He went and I stayed, but I wish I had joined him. It would have been a brilliant adventure. I often wonder now if I'll ever have another opportunity to live that close to a beach.

But almost every decision I've made hoping for the best, while still being afraid, has worked in my favor. Told someone I liked them? Terrifying but also so satisfying, especially when the feelings were mutual. Stood up for myself with teachers? I always got the extension or the new group partner or the extra credit. If I buy the outfit that feels like it's a little too much, or take a chance on a drastic hairstyle that makes me feel good, I am almost always complimented incessantly when friends or even strangers see me in the new looks.

When I decided to finally follow my dream and pursue becoming a published author, I was terrified—terrified of being rejected, yes, but mostly of not being good enough at this thing that I wanted so badly. I think because I was older, I was more willing to take chances in a way I hadn't been before—more aware that the only way to reach this goal was to go after it with everything I had. It was also the first time I can remember wanting something so desperately; the risk of failure felt worth it because not even trying would mean I was unsatisfied and unhappy indefinitely. It didn't happen right away, and I was rejected a lot. There are multiple manuscripts filed away on my computer—stories I wrote and loved but that just weren't up to par. But I kept at it until I wrote one that was. I decided, as Michelle Obama puts it, that I *should* be a published author. That was what *should* happen. And then I did everything in my power to make the dream come true.

Your decisions are always yours and no one else's, and more than likely, no matter what you do, you'll accumulate a regret or two the longer you live. But most of the time you have an opportunity to chicken out or to step up. My hope is that you'll choose the latter more often than you don't.

I've seen firsthand that being president doesn't change who you are. It reveals who you are.

—MICHELLE OBAMA,
Democratic National Convention
speech, 2012

WHEN I WAS NINETEEN, I SIGNED UP TO BE an environmental canvasser. I can't even remember what cause it was for now, whether I was attempting to save baby sea turtles or prevent deforestation, but I'd gone to some kind of info session, and the combination of doing something that felt good in a bone-deep way, along with the potential money to be made, sounded too perfect to pass up. So I arrived at an orientation, and went out on the streets for precisely two days before I realized how incredibly demoralizing it was to constantly ask busy people to stop and listen to me, to care about something they clearly didn't care about, and then to give me, a perfect stranger, their money to put a tiny dent in some massive problem happening on the other side of the world. I thought that doing good shouldn't feel so terrible. Needless to say, I quit.

I quickly found another job that summer—I went to the mall and filled out half a dozen applications and was hired to work in a store called Hollister about two weeks later. If you're unfamiliar with the brand, it's owned by Abercrombie & Fitch, and it's a California-based company packaging and selling clothes that embody that beachy lifestyle to landlocked, preppy, and mostly white teens and young adults everywhere.

It was a cool enough store to work in, mostly because of the other kids I worked with. We were all in high school, recent grads, or in our first or second years of college, and we liked to goof around to make the day pass more quickly. We'd toss the fitting room keys around like a football, try on outfits that were way too big or small when things were slow, and chill in the stockroom—sometimes there was a guitar back there, and the boys were eager to show the girls where to put their fingers on the frets; which strings to pluck for which notes. Sometimes we even had deep, soul-searching talks while we folded jeans. The store had its quirks, like the absurdly low lighting, the fans we were required to spray perfume into every hour or so, and the digital jukebox that we loaded up with songs at the start of our shifts so that we all knew the whole catalog by heart and everyone's favorites by midsummer. But the one weird thing about working there was that every employee stole.

Let me be clear: I'm almost certain no one who worked there needed to steal to, like, *survive.*

I could be wrong, but as far as I know, these weren't struggling single parents or dropouts trying to make ends meet or even people living outside their parents' homes with rent or bills to pay. They were a lot like me: middle- or upper-middle-class students. They could afford to shop there if they wanted the clothes that badly, especially with the employee discount. But the store was a new installment in the mall, so there were no security cameras. And because the store was less than six months old that summer, they had never done inventory. For months, all summer, everyone (and I mean everyone) stole jeans, shirts, shoes, or jackets. Everyone except me.

I don't think I was afraid of getting caught. So many kids had been getting away with it, they had it down to a science. And I can't say that I was overtly aware of the racial politics that may have come into play if I, or any of the other Black or brown kids, *were* caught, versus what might happen to the white kids. But I knew enough to know there was something different in the way the kids who chose to steal moved through the world. They acted like they owned it. I knew I didn't. I'd been taught to work for what I wanted, dumb statement tees and ripped jeans included.

I think I also just felt, deep in my bones, that it was wrong. That I would disappoint my parents. That I would feel ashamed if I were to do it and anyone I respected or loved found out. I'm pretty sure I told my mom the other kids were stealing. I found it kind of funny and didn't really judge them for it. And it was interesting, because they didn't judge me for *not* doing it either. No one called me a Goody Two-shoes or anything. I still got invited to the house parties they had every weekend. I kept in touch with a few of my coworkers for years after. It was weird to see girls I'd witnessed skillfully removing sensors from tank tops and stuffing them into backpacks, then years later holding the hands of their fiancés or their curly-haired toddlers. I just knew the stealing wasn't something I had any interest in doing, and, not to get all after-school special on you, but they respected my choice.

I don't say any of this to brag. In fact, in retrospect, knowing some of the things I know now about Abercrombie & Fitch as a company makes me wish I *did* shoplift that summer. That I could have helped put a tiny dent in a company that has some pretty overtly racist and exclusionary policies kinda makes me want to rewind the clock.

Unlike my former Hollister coworkers, Michelle Obama thinks and talks a lot about values. About knowing who you are and how complicated or unexpected circumstances can reveal so much more about your core belief system than average, everyday experiences because, in a way, you're being tested. I don't think working at a clothing store for a summer is some massive, meditative moment that deserves a ton of attention—it is of course absolutely nothing like becoming the president of the United States—but I do think about that summer a lot. I do think it says something about who I am: that when I was nineteen, a bit of a pushover, and so deeply desperate to be accepted, I didn't do the easy thing. I ruminate over what stopped me from taking what wasn't mine when I had so many opportunities to. And I think that at the end of the day, all it was, all it *is*, is a gut feeling, a hard-and-fast knowledge of my core sense of self, as well as a series of ongoing decisions. It was simple: I didn't want to be someone who stole.

So far, I've been lucky enough to not need to steal, and I still don't want to. It's nothing like being president, this set of three and a half months nearly twenty years ago that didn't affect anyone at all except me. Even still, sometimes when I think about it—that I was tested and that I didn't break—I feel oddly proud.

Our fates are inextricably bound.
If the least of us struggles,
we all in some way feel that pain.

—MICHELLE OBAMA,
Instagram, 2020

THERE HAVE BEEN SO MANY MOMENTS IN MY
life when I've found myself unable to breathe.

I have anxiety, but as I've mentioned, I'd never even heard that word before I became a therapy-going adult. When the panic attacks would seize me, making me gasp for air as I sobbed uncontrollably, as I thought I was dying or seconds away from having a heart attack, I would be terrified, certain the lack of oxygen would be the end of me.

I have asthma, but I thought I'd outgrown it. After a particularly gnarly bout with bronchitis, it returned one spring without my realizing what had happened. I spent months coughing so hard my voice went hoarse and I was wheezing so loudly I could hear it in my own ears. I pointlessly pressed cough drops against the roof of my mouth with my tongue, hoping for relief that never came and misunderstanding that the heaviness in my chest, my ongoing fatigue, and my recurring sinus infections (followed by more bronchitis) meant my lungs were starving.

I am also no stranger to pain. I had recurring ear infections for years as a toddler and young kid until finally, at seven, I had surgery to stop them. My menstrual cramps were so severe that they would always leave me out of commission and would sometimes make me so ill I'd vomit. I would later discover that I had endometriosis: a complicated disorder that causes tissue similar to the tissue in your uterus to grow outside it. The main symptoms are heavy bleeding and severe pelvic pain, but it can also cause scarring on and in your baby-making organs (ovaries and fallopian tubes), which sometimes, though not always, can cause problems if you want to make a baby. I have scoliosis: a curvature of the spine that required me to wear a back brace for sixteen hours a day for two whole years, and while I wore that brace, I also had braces on my teeth. My overbite meant that in addition to braces, I also had to wear headgear—a medieval-looking device that hooked into my braces and protruded out of my mouth. In my thirties, I gave birth without receiving any pain medication until the last possible moment, right before it was time to push. All these things hurt in varying degrees of severity. All these things are a part of me, but they are not who I am.

So far in this book I've told you a few funny

stories and a few serious ones. Maybe there have been a couple of essays where you saw your own experiences or your friends' or (God forbid) your parents' in the lines of my written words. And while I really do hope you laugh at my funny stories and that any experiences we might have in common make you feel less alone, the only real goal I have in writing this book—the only real takeaway I need you to leave this book with—is the knowledge that you are inherently valuable. That you deserve love and acceptance. That you deserve to breathe easily, to live, and to exist simply because you already do. That your life matters.

When I think about the quote above, taken from Michelle Obama's Instagram in one of the only public statements she's ever made about the Black Lives Matter movement and the epidemic of police brutality perpetrated against Black bodies, I think a lot about breath. I think about how much more prevalent asthma and anxiety are in the Black community, largely because of systemic oppression that includes limited access to health care and ingrained biases health providers have, housing discrimination, and the emotional and physical distress that come from existing in a Black body in a country that has long deemed Black bodies as less than human. I think about the real, physical pain of racism, and how it is metaphorically, and sometimes literally, choking all of us, impeding progress, and the way it shows up in every aspect of everyday life in America. I think about how I've always known that Black lives matter, regardless of what this country's history, current events, or white supremacy would have me believe. But when that statement and the sentiment behind it became a movement, things began to shift a bit in my mind and in the way I moved through the world.

People often say "I can't imagine" when something unspeakable happens. But I *can* imagine becoming a victim of police violence, specifically and terrifyingly. When it was reported that George Floyd (like Eric Garner and so many before him) had pleaded that he couldn't breathe again and again as he was being murdered, I viscerally recalled the choke of anxiety; the grip asthma so often had on my own lungs. I remembered all my worst pain—and the feeling of helplessness that often came alongside it. I couldn't shake the scariest parts of those moments: the knowledge that, if something didn't change, death could follow. The fact that what happened to him could happen at any moment to me or someone I love if we happen to be in the wrong place at the wrong time; if we happen to upset the wrong person. The ongoing history of atrocities committed against people who look like me is long and overwhelming. I am weary with the weight of it. Maybe I can't feel the crushing weight of an officer's knee on my neck, but I can feel the tightness in my chest, the struggle to get air to where it needs to go. My body has known all kinds of pain, so I can close my eyes and think of the exact quality of that kind of hurt. I can imagine the terror all too well, and I'm intimately acquainted with tears.

"Dominance, even the threat of it, is a form of dehumanization," Michelle once said. And white supremacy, racism, and systemic oppression are some of the most profane and long-lasting legacies of this: "the ugliest form of power."

I imagine that in Officer Derek Chauvin's eyes, George Floyd had ceased to be human, and all the world's greatest atrocities, from holocausts and ethnic cleansings to every kind of slavery and police brutality, have happened and continue to happen simply because dehumanizing lies are presented and accepted as truths.

In many ways, dehumanization begets more dehumanization. Police forces in the southern United States began as slave patrols—as an inherently racist organization focused on terrorizing enslaved Black people. There are so many other problematic issues in the long, messy history of policing, but suffice it to say it is not a surprise that racial issues linger in the modern-day police force. We're all still dealing with the lingering effects of so many horrifying events. Our inherent interconnectedness is a truth that permeates everything.

With our fates being as inextricably bound as they are, we all need to work harder to see each other as human. And though it's difficult to think about George Floyd without remembering the horrific way he died, we need to try our best to see *him*, not his murder. I am not defined by any day or moment or painful experience in my life, and neither are you. He shouldn't be either. He wasn't a martyr. He was human.

George Floyd was an excellent athlete. He excelled at sports from a young age. He loved football and basketball and played both around his neighborhood and in school. When his athletic abilities caught the eye of a nearby university scout, George was offered a scholarship to play college ball. This was an astounding opportunity, as he would be the first in his family to go to college, and a scholarship would be the only way his family could afford to send him. He went, and when the demands of college became overwhelming (an indication of him being ill-prepared as well as an indictment of a system that doesn't always make college campuses very accessible or welcoming to students of color), he returned home after two years, where he went on to work jobs in construction and security. He also became more involved with church and was a bit of a mentor in his community.

George Floyd loved his family. Part of George's hesitation about college was directly related to leaving the family he loved so deeply.

He was especially close to his mother, whom his brother said he would pick up and twirl around in the kitchen, dancing with her whenever their favorite song came on.

George Floyd was a gentle giant. At nearly 6'7", it's not surprising that George had many nicknames over the course of his life. Known primarily as "Big Friendly" or "Big Floyd," George became a staple in his West Texas community, and many people looked up to and respected him. His neighborhood was full of laughter and love, but it was not without its problems. There's a housing project that was home to predominantly Black tenants, and the police presence was incessant. George had his share of run-ins with the police, and spent a few years in prison, before leaving Texas for a fresh start.

He was a father who wanted more for his

children. In Minneapolis, George cleaned up his act and was making strides to improve his life and the lives of his children. When the pandemic hit, like many people, George Floyd lost his job. But he shouldn't have lost his life.

None of these attributes were things Chauvin knew about Floyd in the moment he chose to kneel on his neck. Maybe if he had taken a second to think of George's promising athleticism or his love for his mother or his ability to reinvent himself again and again, he would have remembered that the person he was hurting was a *person*. Maybe if more of us paused to think about who a stranger might be, who they might love, what they might hope for the future, so much of the world's atrocity would cease to be.

"Everyone on earth is carrying around an unseen history," Michelle has said, "and that alone deserves some tolerance." I think we can do better than tolerance. We are infinitely powerful, and I know we can do and be so much more for each other.

George Floyd just wanted to breathe, like we all do. And our fates are inextricably linked with his. I hope we can all begin to see others with more compassion, so we can stop hurting each other. And so we can all begin to breathe a little easier.

SIDE NOTE: ON HUMANITY AND WHO DESERVES IT

Your life matters. Period.

I grew up with a disabled dad in a too-small house with not much money in a starting-to-fail neighborhood, and I also grew up surrounded by love and music in a diverse city in a country where an education can take you far. I had nothing or I had everything.

—MICHELLE OBAMA,

Becoming

YOU'VE PROBABLY GATHERED FROM THE ES-
says you've read so far that I have a pretty colorful medical history.

Years of recurring ear infections, asthma and severe seasonal allergies, anxiety, scoliosis, and endometriosis. I have had to wear braces and headgear, a back brace, and I've had to endure several surgeries. I'm not sure I ever noticed how much this stuff had been a part of my life until I wrote it all down in a list—saw it outside the context of my overall pretty joyful existence.

But if these medical issues were all someone knew about me, they would easily be able to create a narrative around these limited facts. They'd be able to say, with proof, that I was often ill. If they wanted, they could turn my life into a sob story in the same way some news organizations and reporters tried to spin Michelle Obama's background. Stories can be manipulated to serve whatever narrative you choose.

This is something that happens with alarming frequency—the drawing of conclusions with limited information; the assumption that we know all of someone's story because we can see a single part of it.

You are thinking of all the obvious examples of this now, right? A disabled person being praised as a hero, or pitied, when their disabilities are just a part of their life, an aspect of who they are but definitely not all they are. Assumptions that an immigrant who doesn't speak English well isn't educated. Absolutely everything that happened to George Floyd in the moments before and the months after his murder. You may be thinking of stereotypes and how they limit our view of who someone might be, or biases all based on stories we're telling ourselves. All of these things are examples of why we shouldn't try to tell other people's stories. All of these are examples of how little we know and how cautious we should be when making assumptions.

Almost always, this kind of thinking is used to make the person telling the story feel superior. Using flawed framing to tell a story that positions one human in a position of power over another is incredibly dangerous. It's how we got to where we are now—living in a country that thrives on dominance and exclusion; a society that openly values and continues to provide benefits to some groups of people over others.

In *Becoming*, Michelle Obama tells the story of her first date with Barack. Their first date has since become almost a legend, spawning a movie (*Southside with You*) and fodder for countless interviews with the couple over the years—another story spun in various ways based on who was doing the telling. Everyone from lifestyle magazines to serious journalists have covered the day-long adventure: how the duo went to the Art Institute of Chicago, grabbed sandwiches, then headed to a community meeting where Barack had been invited to speak. Michelle was deeply impressed with his ability to command a room, to inspire a group of strangers with just his voice and presence. In Michelle's own words: "He takes off his suit jacket and launches into what I think is the most eloquent discussion about the world as it is, and the world as it should be. And that was it. Really after that day, that was it. I was in love with him."

She writes that at that meeting he asked the audience, "Do we settle for the world as it is, or do we work for the world as it should be?" They all cheered for the latter, as I think we all would too. If we want to remake the world instead of settling for the way it is now, the first step is to get ourselves out of this cycle of making assumptions. We must begin to imagine people complexly.

It feels weird to use another Spider-Man reference, but whenever I think about imagining people complexly, I often think of Donald Glover. Back in 2011, there was an online campaign for Marvel to cast a Black Spider-Man—and many people wanted it to be Donald Glover. As the campaign gained ground, it of course became a debate. There were people who demanded a Black Spider-Man and didn't want to wait any longer for one, and there were people who adamantly did not want to see a Black man playing Spider-Man . . . ever. In an interview where Donald Glover was asked about the "whole Spider-Man thing," he talks about how he started getting a slew of racist hate mail from "nerds" calling him the N-word. It was easy enough for him to shrug off the overt racism. But the letter that stuck with him was one where the writer thought he was being kind.

This guy seemed to be trying not to ruffle feathers and clearly considered himself to be reasoning with Glover. Donald said in the interview that the letter read, "There are just no Black kids like Peter Parker." At this point, Glover looks incredulous and, I'm paraphrasing, but he says something like, "You can't imagine a Black kid who lives in Queens with his aunt and uncle? Who likes science and who takes photography?" The person who sent that email probably didn't have much exposure to Black people in real life. As a result, he was unable to imagine a Black kid who could be like Peter Parker. He'd let the media, and whatever his experience might have been, limit his ability to see people complexly.

Similarly, in Malcolm Gladwell's *Talking to Strangers*, he writes, "We think we can easily see into the hearts of others based on the flimsiest of clues. We jump at the chance to judge strangers. We would never do that to ourselves, of course. We are nuanced and complex and enigmatic. But the stranger is easy. If I can convince you of one thing in this book, let it be this: Strangers are not easy."

Give strangers the same room to "be" that you would want given to yourself. And don't make assumptions about who someone is when you don't know the full breadth of their existence. If we all do that a bit more in our everyday lives, we can stop settling. We can make the world better, and we can start now.

Being successful isn't
about being impressive,
it's about being inspired.

—MICHELLE OBAMA,
Oregon State University
commencement speech, 2012

WHEN I GET AN IDEA FOR A STORY, IT USUALLY goes something like this:

I feel or hear a character in my head. That might sound weird, but I do. Sometimes it sounds like an actual voice. Sometimes it's just their names, appearing out of nowhere. Sometimes it's a question: *What would happen if . . .* Pretty quickly, I know what they're thinking, who they are, and if it isn't immediately apparent what they want, that's what I have to figure out. I usually know almost all there is to know about the characters before I decide what they look like or what the rest of their story will be about. I also have to piece together what it is that is stopping them from achieving their goal.

I decide if the character I have in my head

and the ideas I'm forming around them is a story worthy of writing an entire book when I can see that my character can reach their goal without too much collateral damage. Or, if they must wreak lots of havoc in order to get what they want, they have to grow and change because of the problems they cause. The outcome must be better for them overall, and even if they don't realize it themselves as the book ends, I should be able to tell the story in a way that the reader will. (This is, of course, a very neat description of an extremely chaotic process, but this is basically what happens.)

So far, I've been lucky. With most of my well-developed ideas, or at least the ones I love, I've been able to figure out a way to help my character succeed. I'm able to picture in my head what needs to change about them or their situation, and what steps they need to take to make those changes happen for their goal to be achieved.

Real life is more like my creative process than I'd like to admit—or at least the way we think about real life is. There are things we set our sights on, obstacles that present challenges, and ways to maneuver that will hopefully end in the result we want. We often decide that we will only consider ourselves a success if and when we reach the goals we set out to reach.

But unlike writing a story that works, I don't think success in real life can or should be measured so simply. Because in the same way that writing a book is much messier than my description above, life can bring all kinds of unexpected twists and turns too.

Michelle Obama could read before she turned four. She skipped second grade and was identified as "gifted" in middle school, which meant she was taking courses like French and advanced biology by the age of ten. She attended an elite magnet high school followed by Princeton, followed by Harvard Law. She was a corporate lawyer and then held several positions in the public sector before setting fundraising records with a community-oriented nonprofit. She went on to become a dean at the University of Chicago and then a vice president at the university's hospital. She was also, of course, the first Black First Lady of the United States of America.

By any stretch of the imagination, Michelle Obama is a success. One couldn't build a more "successful" life with even the wildest of imaginations. But there were still so many moments when Michelle Obama has admitted to feeling like a failure; where she has written that she felt unsure of herself or worried she wasn't good enough for something she wanted or had already worked hard to get.

I too have led a life most would consider successful. I was always on the honor roll, even at my competitive high school, and I graduated cum laude from college. I had a long career in one industry, followed by a shift to another one where I'm currently doing well. But I too was full of insecurity, questions, uncertainty. I still wonder if I'll look back on my life and feel "successful."

I acknowledge that I sit in a place of privilege because I have the time and space to think about success beyond monetary value and status. But when I looked like I was "succeeding" at a lot of points in my life, I was actually miserable. High school was rough on my mental health, and if I could do it over again, I'd rather go to a school that was less respected and less academically demanding but where I'd have had more opportunity to make art and read books I actually wanted to read and where I would have had time to enjoy being a teenager. For part of my career, I had a boss who was a terrible manager and who made me second-guess every thought I had. She stifled my creativity, and the entire time I worked with her, I couldn't write at all. And though I wrote multiple books during the pandemic, I will tell you that it was torture. I would have preferred to spend that time resting, hanging out with my family, and in therapy simply processing my personal grief and the ongoing global trauma, without several projects hanging over my head (though I was and am so grateful I had work when so many didn't). We all should have had the space and financial safety net to take that time to collectively and individually mourn. But that's a topic for another essay.

Michelle too has discussed how difficult it was for her to be in largely white spaces so often and for so long—how lonely it was, how overwhelming and isolating it could feel. She so elegantly wrote in *Becoming* that "it's hard to put into words what sometimes you pick up in the ether, the quiet, cruel nuances of not belonging."

This is not to say that reaching a goal should always be comfortable or that difficulty isn't a part of finding success. It's just to emphasize that how something feels is important to note. A challenge is not the same as the weight and pain of feeling unhappy indefinitely. All the money and fame in the world isn't worth your ongoing unhappiness.

I ultimately feel good when I'm writing. When those characters whisper to me, I feel inspired and excited to find their stories and to tell them. I feel even better when I *finish* writing something, and I think that's an example of a healthier relationship with success: This might be tough, but it will be worth it. If whatever you're working toward no longer feels worth it, it's time to take a look at how you're defining success and to examine your life and your process to see if there's another way to achieve your goal. Remember how I said my characters have to be able to reach their goals without wreaking too much havoc? You should never be your own collateral damage on the way to becoming a success.

Setting goals and working toward them is important. It gives our lives shape and our actions purpose. But reaching those goals can't be the only things we're thinking about as we move through the world. Our definitions of success are too narrow. We have to remember that there is no reader in the story of our real lives. We have to be able to build success in a way that feels good to us, whether it impresses others or not.

Inspiration on its own
was shallow; you had to back
it up with hard work.

—MICHELLE OBAMA,
Becoming

I STARTED A BLOG ONCE CALLED NOTEWOR-thy New York. I say I started it because I start lots of things all the time—I'm someone who is almost always inspired to *start*. And as you know from an earlier essay, I tend to be a bit of a quitter. Still, I've had dozens of hobbies for a week or two, I've started writing (and reading) dozens of books that I never finished, and I've had several blogs on which I only posted a few times. What was notable about Noteworthy New York was that it made me pay closer attention to everyone and everything around me. It quite literally made me look for inspiration.

There is so much noise in New York City, so much tumult. It is so easy to put on my headphones and pull out a book the second I stop moving. Being in public here almost demands that you shut the world out unless you want to be constantly overstimulated. And as someone with anxiety, I usually want to avoid overstimulation at all costs.

Ironically, sometimes doing the opposite of avoiding your triggers is what therapists suggest to manage your anxiety. It's called exposure therapy. Because overstimulation could cause me to panic, it was subtly suggested by my therapist that maybe I should try to shut out the world less—that I should find a way to begin embracing it.

Noteworthy New York was one attempt at this kind of therapy for me. It was a collection of what I called mini-nonfiction, observations I made of things I saw in and around the city that felt noteworthy to me. Here are a few examples of my entries:

Three tiny girls in black sunglasses, wrapped in striped and star-spangled towels, wiggling with excitement as they wait for fireworks.

A mechanic with oil-stained hands using an old straw to tease an orange kitten, in the shadows of his open garage.

A subway performer playing drums with a baby in his lap, the drumsticks in her hands, her hands in his.

A guy wearing red Beats headphones singing reggae out loud like he's in his own bedroom, on the L train.

They were tiny, missable moments, but moments I was inspired to write down. I let the world in little by little, and the grounding exercise of making these observations did help me stay present and panic less in overwhelming situations. Which was why I thought this blog might be one that stuck. In addition to being good for me, it was the embodiment of inspiration: I was writing down things that inspired me to notice. I thought maybe these moments could inspire someone else.

But this blog, like so many other things I've been inspired to start, didn't last. I stayed present by making note of these kinds of moments for a week or two and then I stopped noticing. Or if that isn't generous enough to my past self, I stopped writing about the stuff I was noticing. I was no longer inspired, so I let the project die. And this, I think, is the danger of putting too much emphasis on inspiration itself.

There is nothing inherently wrong with inspiration. Nothing harmful about looking to the works of others or at role models as examples, or even looking out the window if you're feeling stuck in the art you're trying to create or the life you're trying to build. I'd even argue that it is only human to look outside ourselves—to find a specific muse in and for a specific moment. So it isn't surprising that this subject is what authors and artists of all sorts are most frequently asked about: "What was your inspiration for writing/painting/making this?" We're used to it, but I've grown to hate it. Because it misses the point of art, of life. It misses that inspiration is only a tiny piece of the puzzle.

When I first became a professional author, I loved answering this question. I would regale the interviewer or audience with the stories of all the events that led to a particular scene, or the backstories from my real life that colored my characters. I used to love the way people's eyes would light up, or how they'd sit up a little farther in their seats, riveted. But if you're a writer or an artist or hope to become someone who creates things, let me be the one to tell you: This is the part of creativity that everyone romanticizes, even the artists themselves—the spark of the idea. The moment when the magic begins.

The question itself is a little lazy, if you think about it. Because yes, inspiration is interesting, but it's also misleading. People get ideas all the time, and because we're all so obsessed with inspiration, we assume that if we have an idea, it means something profound. But most ideas aren't great ones. Most aren't even very good. Which makes inspiration the least important part of writing a book or making a piece of art. And a moment, no matter how brilliant, does not make a masterpiece.

Writing a book, much like being a part of the First Family, is, in a word . . . difficult. It is great to be inspired by other writers' work, or moments in history, or even your role models' lives, but it's important to remember that inspiration is only the beginning.

I won't pretend to know the intimate details of what a day in the life of the president or First Lady might have been like, but I can tell you exactly what it's like to write a book.

Imagine a book as a fully grown, flowering plant. Maybe a thorny rosebush or a blossoming orange tree. I don't know enough about plants to give you a specific one to think of, so just pick your favorite. The well-drawn characters of your novel are the fruits, the flowers. The side characters are the buds, maybe a few of the leaves. The setting and plot are the branches or stems, and the conflict is the soil. The inspiration, in the case of this metaphor, would be the seed. The seed is obviously important, because it is where the plant starts. But the seed itself is not what makes the plant grow into its fullest and most fruitful form.

When people buy plants, they rarely ask what the seeds look like. They ask how often the plant needs to be watered, if it should sit by a window or if it thrives better in the shade. They ask about the work it takes to keep the plant alive—how best to make it beautiful.

Life is like this too, right? Of course where and how you start matters—it helps to shape who you are, for better or worse. But once you're in a position to start making your own choices, once you have the opportunity to plant yourself in good or better soil, to give yourself what you need to thrive, everything can change. The seeds of your life aren't nearly as important as what you try to do with them.

As a writer, it is my job to make sure I don't just gather seeds. I have to plant my seeds in good soil, protect them from stormy weather, and give them the sun they need to thrive. I must take care of my little inspiration seeds so that they grow and bloom. And that hard work is what matters more than the seed itself. I've started plenty of blogs and books but only brought a few of them to full fruition. So think of anything you want to make, from art to the life you're currently creating for yourself, in the same way. It is less about how it started, and more about the commitment you have to make it into something beautiful.

I am an example of what is possible
when girls from the very beginning of
their lives are loved and nurtured by
people around them. I was surrounded by
extraordinary women in my life who taught
me about quiet strength and dignity.

—MICHELLE OBAMA,
address to Elizabeth Garrett Anderson
students, 2011

I LOVE MICHELLE OBAMA. I THINK THAT'S clear from the existence of this book alone. And I think lots of girls and women can and should aspire to be more like her. But when I read the quote above, I thought immediately of another quote by Tressie McMillan Cottom, one of my other go-to role models, and in my opinion one of the greatest thinkers of our time: "Smart is only a construct of correspondence between one's abilities, one's environment, and one's moment in history." While in this instance Tressie was talking about how arbitrary "smartness" can be, what it illustrates applies to so many other parts of our lives on macro and micro levels: Our success is a product of so many factors, but most importantly, who we are and how our circumstances either amplify or diminish our natural gifts.

I, like Michelle, did have this experience, and I credit my mother, father, and several other influential and positive adults in my life for where I've landed and how things have turned out. But I also know and understand that plenty of people haven't had the privilege of being loved and nurtured by everyone around them.

If I'm describing your experience—if you're perhaps a person who is brilliant but lacking resources, or who needs extra help that isn't available, or if you're doing it all for everyone else but lacking a support system of your own—there is still hope. At the back of this book is a list of all kinds of resources: books and organizations; practical things, people, and places that give you hope and help you find extraordinary people who will pour into your life in the way the women in Michelle's life did for her, the way my parents and family and friends did for me. I honestly believe what Michelle says so often, that if she can do what she's done, anyone can. But I do think there's nuance to that statement. Anyone can do it with the right circumstances, the right information, confidence, and the mix of preparation and opportunity. I will do what I can to help with the information part of that equation. The rest is up to you, your belief in yourself, your circumstances, and your willingness to work toward an uncertain future. I may not know everything, but of these things I am certain: We are no different from you. You deserve everything you want. You are worthy of love and acceptance. And if I, an anxious, procrastination-prone new mom in the middle of a global pandemic, can finish a book by a random deadline, anything is possible.

SIDE NOTE: ON BEING GOOD ENOUGH

You are.

Lead by example with
hope; never fear, and know that I
will be with you, rooting for you and working
to support you for the rest of my life.

—MICHELLE OBAMA,
final remarks as First Lady, 2017

IN THE VERY FIRST NATIONAL SPEECH BARACK

Obama ever gave (and in nearly every speech after) he spoke endlessly of hope.

On July 27, 2004, Barack Obama wasn't a name many had heard before, but that—and the then-campaigning state senator's life—was about to change.

On that day in Boston, at the Democratic National Convention, Barack was set to deliver the keynote address, and Michelle was nervous. She was nervous even though she knew Barack was ready for this. He'd practiced the speech for hours over the course of the last several weeks—practiced it so much, in fact, that Michelle knew he'd be reciting the entire thing from memory and ignoring the provided teleprompters, depending as he usually did on his own mind over anything else.

Even with this knowledge, and the knowledge that her husband was always calm under immense pressure (a trait that would serve him well in the years to come), she felt antsy waiting in the wings. She could feel something starting when he let go of her hand and stepped out into the bright stage lights—something big.

The speech was both an introduction and an inspiration—it was the first time the world was hearing Barack's origin story and the first time half of the country fell in love with him. In front of millions, Barack spoke of his humble background, of being the child of a Kenyan and a Kansan, of how his story—his *life*—wouldn't have been possible in any other country on earth. And how his existence and his presence there onstage was the embodiment of the American Dream.

He was onstage for seventeen minutes, and in that short time he received a half dozen standing ovations from the packed convention center. In less than half an hour, he inspired the thousands who shared that room with him and the millions more who were watching from home. He made us hope. He made us believe change was possible. He made us want to do good and he made us want to be better.

At one point, near the end of his address, Barack Obama insisted that the politics of hope was not blind optimism or willful ignorance. Hope was what gave enslaved people the vigor to sing freedom songs. Hope was what inspired immigrants to set out for foreign lands full of possibility. Hope was what made him believe that there was a place for him in this country, and more importantly, that he could make a difference. And that hope, he said, was what America needed to hold on to in the months and years to come.

In the days that followed, it seemed that he'd made quite the impression. There was talk, almost instantly, of how he could be the first Black president of the United States.

Michelle joined her husband onstage that night when he'd spoken the final words of his keynote, wrapped him in a hug, and stood in awe of the roaring crowd. "Must have been a good speech," Michelle whispered to him then, and she would repeat the sentiment as a joke with him later, every time some unexpected opportunity arose or whenever a stranger recognized them on the street. And a good speech it was. That moment, they both know now, was the first time they made history. It was the beginning of everything.

By the time the Obama campaign was in full swing, the well-known street artist Shepard Fairey had even created a poster with the literal word HOPE emblazoned beneath a stenciled image of Barack, a poster that soon became inextricably linked to the campaign despite being independently created. Even Barack Obama's catchphrase, the slogan that has become synonymous with him, was an embodiment of that hope: *Yes we can.*

It's understandable why so many were so hopeful. Besides Barack and Michelle themselves speaking of it in nearly every public appearance they made, with Barack as the first Black presidential candidate, expectations were high well before the Obamas became the First Family. Their existence was an embodiment of hope for me and countless others. Michelle often talks about feeling like she and Barack and even their children were under a microscope—they couldn't afford to make a mistake. It was impossible for them to relax because there were just as many people expecting them to fail as they had on the side of hope. People hoped that Barack Obama winning the presidency would mean big changes for the country. Perhaps *change* was the only word heard more often than *hope* during Obama's terms. They hoped that a president like Obama would make their everyday lives better. I think some even hoped that electing a Black president would mean something about the country had shifted. Or healed.

While the past few years have proven that we have a long way to go, I still feel that undercurrent of hope, largely because of *you*.

I write for teens and kids because I believe you all are better than my generation is, better than all who have come before us. As a whole, young people now are more tolerant and accepting, more open-minded, more willing to listen and be flexible, and more likely to act (vote, protest, make your voice heard) than ever before. I don't know if it's because the internet and social media are connecting people more and more, providing perspectives and experiences that would otherwise remain obscure, or if the ease with which there is access to information now facilitates deeper and more immediate understanding of the world's atrocities. But for lack of a better phrase: Y'all just built different. You're built better. And the second you're able to recognize and hone your limitless power, your boundless promise, things are going to change. Michelle and I will be working alongside you in any and every way we can.

Things, I can tell, are already changing.

SIDE NOTE: ON BEING THE FIRST

Michelle Obama has said that "making mistakes was not an option" for her and Barack as the first Black POTUS and FLOTUS, but Michelle felt this pressure long before she entered the White House.

Michelle had always stood out—first as a kid who "talked like a white girl" *in* her South Side neighborhood, then as a high achiever at Whitney Young *from* her South Side neighborhood—so she was used to it. And college presented a new, eye-opening, and in some ways more isolating experience for the future First Lady.

She arrived at Princeton's New Jersey campus a few weeks early to attend a preparatory orientation specifically for first-generation, minority, and low-income students. The program was aimed at students like her because they were considered at "high risk" of dropping out and the extra support was meant to help ease them into campus life and hopefully make a successful transition.

She enjoyed the program and met friends during those first weeks who she would carry with her through the rest of her college career, but once the full student body arrived on campus, she immediately felt out of place. She recalls that she and the other brown and Black students from her orientation felt othered—like "poppy seeds in a bowl of rice." While Michelle would succeed there, Princeton—which was largely white and male—was where she most acutely felt her Blackness and, more importantly, how much her experiences and the color of her skin set her apart in largely white spaces.

Similarly to how she felt responsible for representing the South Side in high school, once she got to college, that pressure expanded so that she often felt she was speaking for her entire race.

She worried that anything she said could be taken out of context and that her place at Princeton would be questioned and doubted—reduced to a result of affirmative action and not her own merit.

Because of this, most of Michelle's friends were also students of color, and she wrote her dissertation on the racial divide on campus. I can only imagine how being thrust into the spotlight further exacerbated the feelings that inspired her dissertation and that followed her to law school, law offices, and into corporate America when her husband won the presidential race.

You might feel a similar kind of pressure, if not because of your race then maybe because of your gender, your socioeconomic background, or even your name. You may be the first person in your family who is college bound, or the first person in your friend group to "make it," and with that comes immense expectations. But this is to let you know that though you're the first, you're not as alone as you might feel.

Let me be clear—that added pressure is not fair. In a perfect world, we would all be judged and treated fairly regardless of who we are. And while I don't want you to feel pressured to be perfect because you happened to be the first, I understand why you might feel that way. Take comfort in the fact that the Obamas were not perfect. They tried their best and were, in my opinion, mostly outstanding. But they were not perfect, because perfection doesn't exist.

There's freedom in being the first too—a chance to change things for the better; to make brave decisions that no one is expecting; to do things people have never thought to do. The Obamas worked to change so many things and upset a lot of people, both their supporters and their dissenters, along the way. But the Obama administration also completely rethought the way this country structures its health-care system, made huge strides in several international relationships (perhaps most notably with Cuba), and inspired hope in a time when the citizens of the United States desperately needed it. If nothing else, they disrupted the establishment just by virtue of who they were. They asked new questions even when they didn't have all the answers.

It's an honor to be first; to be a trailblazer. To change things so that those who follow might have it a little easier. But it is called trailblazing for a reason. Changing a long-established path might require that the new trail be made of scorched earth. Sometimes burning it all down is the only way to take the world, and yourself, in a new direction.

There's power in allowing yourself
to be known and heard, in owning your
unique story, in using your authentic
voice. And there's grace in being
willing to know and hear others.

—MICHELLE OBAMA,
Becoming

YOU MAY HAVE STARTED READING THIS BOOK

because you think that Michelle Obama is re-markable, and in a lot of ways she obviously is. She came from a humble, working-class family. She prioritized her education. She set goals and then worked tirelessly to reach them. She owned her own story in more ways than one. And she is now building a media empire that aligns with her personal values—she is reaching back and bring-ing others forward with her. But what I hope you take away from this little book of mine is that being remarkable is something that is possible for anyone—not just the Michelle Obamas of the world.

If I can take a few dozen random things that Michelle has said over the years and find deep connections within my own life that align with her words and experiences, so can you. If Michelle and I can start in one place and end where we have—her with a global audience and a history-making, record-breaking life, and me with several published books and more on the way—so can you. If she has the ability to carve out a life she loves for herself; if I can move in a way that ever so slowly brings me closer to my dreams; if you can ask yourself what it is you want and then fearlessly answer, you can do remarkable things too.

Shortly after moving into the White House, Michelle visited an all-girls performing arts school in London where the students put on a show. She'd been feeling unmoored by her new position as First Lady and unsure of what she would do, who she would become. But in that moment, as she watched the girls perform, she wrote that she saw her purpose very clearly. "It was a strange, quiet revelation: They were me, as I'd once been. And I was them, as they could be." Michelle was you. Michelle was me. And we can become the best versions of ourselves the same way she did.

One of the most magical things about stories is that there can be someone on the other side of the world, with a completely different background, whom you feel you have nothing in common with but who somehow feels or has felt exactly as you do at any given moment, just as Michelle saw herself in the Black and brown girls at the school in London. I hope this book shows you that too: that if I can see myself in Michelle's words and experiences, maybe you can see your-self in mine. We're never truly alone, if only we have the patience to listen to the stories of others, and the courage to share our own.

AFTERWORD

AS I SAID AT THE START OF THIS BOOK, I, LIKE nearly everyone else in the world, have no idea what I'm doing. It's totally okay if you don't either. While it may seem scary that no one has all the answers and that there aren't any quietly kept secrets about how to best live your life, perhaps the opposite is also true. There's bravery in discovering what feeds your body and mind. There's comfort in the knowledge that your life is yours to live as you choose. There's power in those choices and hope in every decision you make, and there's an abundance of joy to be found just as often as you may be faced with confusion or pain.

And role models like Michelle Obama are there to help us through it all.

Because of this, I won't use this afterword to make any grand declarations. But I do hope you consider keeping a few of Michelle's most astute bits of wisdom in mind:

Stand by your values. Even when everyone around you is falling into easy rhythms or sacrificing their sense of self for acceptance or inclusion. It will make your life richer, your relationships stronger, and your character something to be proud of.

We are all connected. If one of us is oppressed or hurting, the progress of our society and our collective future will suffer. In everything you do, work to ensure your fellow humans are safe and that their lives and contributions are valued.

Be inspired and work hard. Seek to make ambitious goals for yourself and work toward them, but don't forget to notice and appreciate the beauty all around you. There is value in both the moments of inspiration and everything that comes after.

You were born worthy. You are worthy of love and acceptance and everything else you want and need from this life. You are worthy of all these things not because of who you are or where you're from or the things you've done, but simply because you exist.

A few of my other favorites: **Own your story. Friendship matters. Never stop becoming the best version of yourself.**

But perhaps the one piece of Michelle's advice that I hope stays with you forever is this:

Never be afraid to fail. Don't be afraid to jump at unexpected opportunities, to take a chance, to try something new. Don't be afraid to open your eyes underwater, because even if you never find the ring at the bottom of the pool, you'll have seen the world in a way you never expected. You'll learn that, like Michelle's early days in high school and college and even in the White House, sometimes the scariest moments in our lives are the ones that show us who we are.

RESOURCES

GIRLS' ORGANIZATIONS

- Girls Going Global
- Girls Inc.
- Girls Rock Camp Alliance
- Girls Who Code
- Girls Write Now
- Radical Monarchs
- SheJumps

LGBTQ ORGANIZATIONS

- The Audre Lorde Project
- Gender Diversity
- Gender Proud
- Gender Spectrum
- GLSEN
- It Gets Better Project
- The Trevor Project
- Trans Lifeline
- Trans Youth Equality Foundation

THERAPY ORGANIZATIONS

- The Loveland Foundation Therapy Fund

- True Colors United

- Therapy for Black Girls

- National Queer & Trans Therapists of Color Network

- Open Path Collective

- Black Female Therapists

- The Local Optimist Hotline,

- Crisis Text Line

BOOKS

- *Becoming*, Michelle Obama

- *Yes She Can*, compiled by Molly Dillon

- *Thick*, Tressie McMillan Cottom

- *Talking to Strangers*, Malcolm Gladwell

- *Quiet Power*, Susan Cain

- *Shout*, Laurie Halse Anderson

- *Stamped: Racism, Antiracism, and You*, Jason

Reynolds & Ibram X. Kendi

- ***Secret Garden: An Inky Treasure Hunt and Coloring Book,*** Johanna Basford
- ***Good Days Start With Gratitude*** (gratitude journal)
- ***Hope Nation***, edited by Rose Brock (and others)
- ***Anxiety Relief for Teens***, Regine Galanti
- ***The Little Book of Mindfulness***, Dr. Patrizia Collard

ACKNOWLEDGMENTS

To my agent, Beth Phelan: Thank you for everything, always.

To my parents: Thank you for your unending support. For reading everything I write. For being my personal cheerleaders, my biggest fans, my greatest joys.

To Cass: Thank you for taking the baby away from me, sometimes by force. And for always bringing me plates of food and doughnuts and cups of coffee and glasses of wine.

To my Macmillan family, and especially to Jean and Anna: Thank you for giving me years of happiness at work—such a rare and wondrous thing. And for your undying patience, generous flexibility, and for always believing in me once I became one of your authors instead of one of your colleagues. I'm so proud to be published by you.

NOTES